Messianic Theology and Christian Faith

Messianic Theology and Christian Faith

by

George A. Riggan

THE WESTMINSTER PRESS
Philadelphia

PUBLISHED BY THE WESTMINSTER PRESS®
PHILADELPHIA, PENNSYLVANIA

PRINTED IN THE UNITED STATES OF AMERICA

To
Todd and Lora Wheeler

Contents

Preface

The following chapters expand the content of lectures first delivered in Okinawa, Japan, and Korea at retreats conducted in the fall of 1961 for Protestant chaplains serving U.S. Armed Forces in the Far East. The same lectures, modified in the give-and-take of those colloquies, were later delivered on several occasions to groups of laymen in this country. Some of their content has been used in the classroom.

This book is written chiefly for informed and questing laymen and for college students. It aims to serve the need of the nonprofessional student for an introduction to scholarly research, the results of which are common knowledge in professional theological circles, and the implications of which are momentous for an understanding of theological phenomena. It aims further to guide him to more technical literature at the points of his own interest. In these respects, it may prove useful as well to ministers and other professional readers who wish to review some of the issues considered.

This writing has been done in the growing conviction that the informed layman has neither the need nor the desire to be shielded from the stark formulations of the findings and questions which currently engage the scholarly community in theology. It presupposes that when he is accepted as a partner in the contemporary theological dialogue, the layman can make an invaluable contribution to the reconstruction of faith and life in religious community. This work itself is concerned with one of the central questions of that dialogue: What has it meant historically that a man was called the Messiah, and by implication, What does it mean to be a Christian?

The research underlying the writing has served a personal and professional need to examine controversial issues in contemporary theology against the background of current critical studies in Judeo-Christian literature. I have received as a dividend a more intimate acquaintance with the writings of Biblical scholars whose work is indispensable to my own, but in whose fields I have no professional competence. My debt to them, acknowledged in many ways in the following pages, is here expressly remembered with gratitude.

The competent critic will note omissions of important literature relevant to the subject in hand. Selections have been made, both from traditional literature and from current scholarly studies, with a concern, first, for the historical origins of controversial issues in contemporary messianic theology, and second, for the layman's interest in pursuing his particular questions in the more readily accessible technical studies.

Scripture references are from the Revised Standard Version, with the exception that the word " Messiah " has been substituted for the word " anointed."

My gratitude also extends to the faculty and students of The Hartford Seminary Foundation for the many ways in which their labors in our common enterprise have contributed to my own work. I am especially grateful to Profs. Wilhelm Wuellner, Richard Weingart, and Harvey McArthur for their contributions to this project, though I hasten to absolve them of all responsibility for the outcome. Indebtedness is gratefully acknowledged as well to my wife, for encouragement and candid criticism, and to Miss Alice Barlow for the meticulous typing of a manuscript the stylistic eccentricities of which remain at my insistence and over her protest.

G. A. R.

Hartford, Connecticut

Chapter I

Messianic Kingship in Ancient Israel

In its earliest flowering Hebraic messianism on its human side embodied an imperialist vision of Hebrew world dominion. This vision found an institutional expression in the pretensions and practices of divine kingship, a socioreligious arrangement borrowed by the nomadic Hebrews from their Oriental neighbors during the period of their conquest of Canaan (Palestine).

The claim that kingship was a form of messianism here rests simply upon the fact that from the beginning of the monarchy until it ceased, anointment by a priest served in both Northern and Southern Israel as the indispensable sociocultic foundation and legitimation of the king's rule. The term " messiah " in its Hebrew form, *mashiach,* as well as in the Aramaic, *meshicha,* and the Greek, *christos,* is simply a verbal adjective meaning " anointed " (with oil). A Hellenized spelling of the Aramaic, *messias,* is the source of our English words " messiah " and " messianic." Numerous, as we shall see, were the Hebrew cult uses of anointment — customs likewise borrowed from the Canaanites. Yet in Hebrew literature the unqualified phrase, " messiah of Yahweh," is exclusively a synonym for the king or for the whole Davidic dynasty until after the exile into Babylonia in 597 B.C. It follows that the theology interpreting such kingship is also a sort of theological messianism, however mistaken some of its content may prove to have been.

The definitive concern of theology is the act or word of God — God's coming to expression. Thus the theologian, however moved or unmoved he may be by what God is actually doing, is at least about his proper work in giving his account of God's action. As this present study intends to be primarily theological, it follows that the social history of Israel, even more specifically its cult history, is here of only incidental concern. Yet Hebrew theology, and especially Hebraic messianism, tenaciously held that God's recurrent coming to expression as God for man is an event historically mediated. Consequently, it is our preliminary thesis that the empirical failure of Hebrew messianic royalism, in theological theory no less than in social praxis, was received by the community as divine revelation and the occasion for a reformulation of messianic theology.

We need not be theologically embarrassed, therefore, by massive shifts in the sociotheological content of the Hebrew term *mashiach* from its use to designate the actual king in ancient Israel to its use in Judaism after the exile to denote a heavenly figure whose coming was expected to bring the end (*eschaton*) of the present age. Further, the absence of eschatology from the ideology of kingship is no adequate cause for insisting that the word " messianic " is misused when applied to Israel's kings.[1] Eschatological expectations are the new element in reconstructed messianism, received in turn as the medium of further revelation.

THE BEGINNINGS OF KINGSHIP IN ISRAEL

Divine kingship, arising in the Near East around the fourth millennium B.C., and later borrowed by Israel from her neighbors, was a radical sociotheological breakthrough in mass organization for war and for the production and distribution of goods. In the Sumerian, Egyptian, Old Babylonian, and Assyrian models, e.g., royalism was effectively an interlocking system of social machines, built by conscription or enslavement of interchangeable and replaceable human parts, comprising military armies, work armies, and a complex bureaucracy under the central control of a king. As the core of the totalitarian system, the king was considered a god (by the Egyptians) or an indispensable divine mediator of heaven's blessings (by the Sumerians, Babylonians, etc.),[2] whose godlike will was life or death and whose power while it lasted was practically, if not always ideologically, absolute.

The several royalist complexes typically controlled a constellation of existing technologies ranging from writing, astronomy, and mathematics to metallurgy, engineering, and military science. Yet more by ruthlessly organized waste of human life and energy than by technological innovation, the civil and military armies of royalism lifted human construction and destruction alike to levels before inconceivable. Thus by its very constitution royalism variously injured the human condition: by ruthless physical coercion, by paranoid measures against revolt and usurpation, by ingrained aggression against neighboring people, by inherent destructiveness and instability.

The Hebrews won their long struggle for possession of Palestine — essentially a contest between a vigorous, nomadic people and a number of decadent royalist systems — but they won only at the eventual cost of adopting and adapting the royalist system into their own nomadic ethos.

Their first opponents were the Canaanites, otherwise identifiable as the Hyksos, who ruled Egypt from around 1700 to 1550 B.C., at which time they were finally expelled and their empire in Palestine and Syria taken over by the Pharaohs. Even the beginnings of the invasion under Joshua were possible, in part, because of the corruption and indifference of Egyptian overlords; in part, because of the fragmentation of the Canaanite vassal empire into an increasing number of feudal kingdoms precariously holding the land adjacent to fortress cities such as Jerusalem. In the period of the Judges, competition with other invading nomads — the Midianites, for example — further complicated their military situation. The Philistines (Phoenicians), however, proved to be their stoutest foe, threatening not only the further invasion of the land by the Hebrews, but their very own existence as an independent people. The Philistines, part of a larger migration originating in the Aegean

Islands, had fallen back into coastal Palestine after an abortive invasion of Egypt. The Hebrew royal dynasty dates from the Philistine crisis.

Hebrew technology of the premonarchic period stood in sharp, though ever diminishing, contrast with that of the Canaanites and Philistines. The Hebrews were long unable to conquer the Palestinian plains, because their foot soldiers were ineffective against the Canaanite war chariots, except in the hill country. (Josh. 17:16; Judg. 1:19; 4:2 f.) True, they had slowly acquired from their neighbors the rudiments of agriculture, pottery-making, bronze metallurgy, and the like. But the technology of the iron age, introduced among the Canaanites by the Philistines, was apparently kept from the Hebrews as a military secret until after David and Solomon made good with weapons of bronze their dreams of a pan-Palestinian Hebrew monarchy. Yet Israel's greatest debt to foreign technology was the institution itself of royalty — one might almost say, of government. " In those days there was no king in Israel; every man did what was right in his own eyes." (Judg. 21:25.) Until the establishment of the monarchy, there existed in Israel no authority to levy taxes, or to conscript labor, or to muster armies and keep them in the field.

Premonarchic Israel was not, in the precise technical sense, a political entity. Neither was Yahwism, in our current meaning, a religion. Israel was then an amphictyony — a loose coalition of neighboring tribes for the perpetuation of a cultus and the defense of its central site. Yahwism was a war cult, the relevance of which was in no dispute among a people long bent upon conquest and successful occupation. The fluid and variable cohesion of the cult can be judged from the fact that there existed among the Hebrews two amphictyonies, one embracing all twelve tribes and centering at Shechem in Northern Israel (later at Shiloh), another embracing only six of the tribes and centering at Hebron in Southern Israel.

The initiative in her conquest of Canaan, as in all matters determining her existence, Israel ascribed to Yahweh — a characteristic expression of her sense of being a people of historical destiny. According to cultic ideology, Yahweh's special guardianship was exercised through cosmic no less than through historical events. Our present concern, however, is Hebrew understanding of Yahweh's presence within her own communal religious behavior, here defined in its broad totality as cultus, for this is the historical matrix within which the institution of monarchy developed. This procedure, moreover, is thoroughly consonant with Israel's own characteristic self-understanding, for in referring ultimate initiative to Yahweh she was mindful of the historical agents through whom she perceived Yahweh to act.

We have in fact no clear picture of the amphictyonic cultus or of its functionaries; our records date from the period of the monarchy. Yet several cultic activities do emerge as media of Yahweh's presence, among them ritual, oracle, and holy war.

Human behavior in these pursuits might follow the highly stylized performance of a cult official, governed by tradition; it might follow the spontaneous improvization of a charismatic enthusiast; or it might follow some fusion of the two. Just how impersonal office with its prescribed routine was related in the cultus to personal charisma with its incalculable freedom is no longer certain. Yet clearly each was taken as a medium of Yahweh's coming to expression, subservient alike to his personal will, dispensable at his pleasure.[3]

Ritual, viewed simply as human work, played a central role in the perpetuation and interpretation of cultic ideology. Viewed in its own theological terms, ritual was a medium through which Yahweh recurrently prolonged a special relationship with his chosen people. Chief among the rituals of Yahwism, celebrated regularly at its cult site in Shiloh, was the great harvest festival, to which members from all the tribes made annual pilgrimage. The liturgy involved the offering of sacrifice, but the features peculiar to Yahwism were the confession of Yahweh as God, the remembrance of his acts in the history of Israel, the hearing of his law and subscribing to it in the recitation and prolongation of the covenant made between him and his people at Sinai.

Oracle was the means whereby Yahweh's will for current

crises was specified. The oracle might take the form of a dream, a sign event, the manipulation of Urim and Thummim by a priest, or the ecstatic utterance of a prophet. Prophetic oracle, nascent in premonarchic Israel, was destined to be a decisive factor in the cultus during the monarchy.

In holy war, undertaken only when the vital interests of the amphictyony as a whole were at stake, Israel perceived the special guardianship of Yahweh. Ritual preparation and taboos surrounded its conduct, but the call to arms and leadership in battle was the prerogative of the military hero. The hero's leadership was understood and accepted by the people as a spontaneous charisma — a special gift manifesting the outpouring of Yahweh's Spirit. Under the impulse of that Spirit, he fought with a fanatic enthusiasm, awe-inspiring to his friends and terrifying to his enemies.

In the phase of the conquest prior to the monarchy, the so-called " judges " epitomized the military hero. Just why these men were called judges is a matter of continuing speculation. Apparently they had nothing to do with the ordinary administration of justice, which was left to the elders of the several tribes. Their office was apparently concerned only with the justice and judgment of Yahweh — that is to say, with matters affecting the sacral bond between Yahweh and the amphictyony as a whole. From an examination of Judg. 3:10, von Rad concludes that sacral judgment might consist in a warlike act, with the meaning " to help one get what one is due." On that basis he advances the thesis that " the judges were men whom Yahweh raised up in order through them to prove the justice of his dealings with his people." [4]

The charisma of the military hero, and of the judge in particular, was not an endowment permanently associated with the office or a heritage transmissible from father to son. The gift was personal and short-lived. Yahweh alone could prolong it by renewed breathing of his *ruach* — his breath or Spirit — upon the man. Consequently, in Israel under the judges, responsibility and authority for practical social decision were weak and widely dispersed because their exercise depended upon popular consent at the time and on the spot. This consent could not be depended upon even under conditions of direct danger. By way of classic illustration, the very ancient Song of Deborah upbraids a number of the tribes for failing to make their appearance at the Battle of Esdraelon — decisive against the Canaanite coalition forces under Sisera (Judg., ch. 5). The later and more lethal challenge of the Philistines, by cruelly exposing the weakness of purely charismatic leadership, contributed to the eventual displacement of the judge by the king.

A most important figure in the transition from amphictyony to monarchy was Samuel, last of the great judges, one of the early prophets, and — by accounts favorable to the Davidic dynasty — a kingmaker in Israel. In his time the Philistines were repeatedly hurling the weight of their power against Israel. Invading Israelite territory from the north, they eventually reached and overran Shiloh, principal seat of Yahwism. Hebron remained as the cult site of the six southern tribes, but with the fall of Shiloh the pan-Hebrew coalition ceased to function as a true amphictyony.

The continuing renewal and realization of the specifically Hebrew ethos had centered in the cultus of the Shiloh shrine. Now demolished was the shrine itself and the city. Captured was the Ark of the Covenant, central symbol of Yahwism at the site. Suspended, at least for a time, was the great annual festival reenacting and prolonging the Yahwist covenant in which were grounded Israel's sense of her continued existence and her hope for the future. Silenced was the festival liturgy in which resounded an early account of the events at Sinai — a copy of which was probably kept in the Ark. Dead was Eli the priest, who for years had reenacted Moses as covenant mediator, speaking to the assembled tribes for Yahweh and in his name, recalling the mighty deeds ascribed to him, proclaiming his promises to Israel, his law, and his rightness. Ended by Eli's death, and by the slaughter of his sons in battle, was the priesthood of the shrine.

Samuel is portrayed as the legitimate successor of Eli the priest (I Sam., ch. 3), presumably in his role as covenant mediator between Yahweh and the whole of Israel. Supposing some authentic historical foundation for this view, we are struck by the fact that Samuel stepped into the role starkly denuded by the Philistines of the sacramental aids traditionally associated with the office at Shiloh. The mediating office of Moses, stripped of Ark and shrine and festival pageantry, he prolonged prophetically [5] rather than liturgically. He no longer spoke to the tribes on one fixed date, but as occasion demanded; no longer from one fixed site, but from the ground upon which he happened to be standing. He remembered Yahweh's mighty deeds of the past as prolonged in the current military action of the cult rather more than in its festival celebration. He spoke to the people for Yahweh and in his name, interpreting his will not so much through cultic and moral law as through concrete decisions in the face of clear and present danger.

As the military crisis mounted, the tribal elders came to Samuel and in the face of his strong opposition demanded a king, " that we also may be like all the nations, and that our king may govern us and go out before us and fight our battles " (I Sam. 8:20). Samuel yielded by anointing first Saul, and later David, as king — with the prevailing understanding that his action was the will, however reluctant, of Yahweh himself. Whether we have here an authentic reflection of Samuel's part in the shift of power or a later reinterpretation by Jerusalem court circles favorable to sacral kingship is a controversial question. The record suggests that he conceived of kingship in Israel as no more than an institutionalized extension of charismatic military leadership. Clearly, he founded no royal dynasty, either in the line of Saul or of David. His anointment of David to the succession of the throne seems possibly to have been a block to Saul's dynastic ambition, essentially a yielding to popular will and a bid for a limited monarchy subservient to his own office as judge and covenant mediator. Saul, at least, never broke with the old order of military heroes or from his dependence upon Samuel. Adaptation and assimilation of the alien traditions of sacral kingship into the Hebrew cultus were chiefly the work of David and Solomon.

Several factors favored David's dynastic ambition and his growing conception of the central role of the monarchy in the life of Israel. First, he began his reign as king of the southern tribes only; for at the death of Saul and Jonathan the coalition of the twelve tribes was split by the question of succession. Saul's heirs ruled the northern tribes. In this period, David held court at Hebron, cult site of the southern subcoalition, in a theological climate more favorable than that of Northern Israel for the assimilation of Canaanite and Hebrew cultures. Second, he captured Jerusalem with no damage to its seemingly impregnable fortifications. In Jerusalem he mounted an existing throne, thereby declaring himself a successor to the ancient priest-king, Melchizedek. Thus he absorbed the Canaanites of the city into his own people and borrowed from the royal traditions of his new subjects to suit his own purposes. Third, after his accession by popular acclamation to the throne of Northern Israel, he led the twelve tribes in subduing all resistance to Hebrew rule in the whole of Palestine. Fourth, he recaptured the Ark of the Covenant and removed it to his capital, Jerusalem. Thus he cemented alien monarchism into the ancient traditions of the cult by making Zion, the City of David, the seat as well of Yahweh's presence in Israel. Despite initial resistance from those defending the Tent of Meeting of desert tradition against royal innovation, his plan to build a house for Yahweh on Zion, carried out by Solomon, eventually brought together palace and Temple in the hearts and imaginations of the people as no military success alone could possibly have done.

LEGITIMATION OF DAVID'S MESSIANIC DYNASTY

David's acceptance as king in Northern Israel was based upon popular consent to a covenant drawn between him and his new subjects. When Solomon succeeded him to the throne, dynastic considerations prevailed; he dispensed with the formality of a covenant with any of the twelve tribes. Upon Solomon's death in ca. 925 B.C., however, Rehoboam failed in his attempt to perpetuate in the whole of Israel a purely dynastic royalism. His refusal to negotiate a covenant acceptable to the ten northern tribes divided the kingdom. Yet even among the ten tribes, monarchy persisted as the form of government until Assyria obliterated Northern Israel in 721 B.C. In the North, however, the king continued to be regarded as a variant of the old military hero; and succession to the throne, often by way of grim political contest, was taken to be a direct gift from Yahweh — a charisma independent of dynastic inheritance. In Southern Israel, as well, royalism was restricted and modified by the ancient traditions of Yahwism, but far less so than in the North. Especially significant is the fact that in the South inheritance of the throne in the lineage of David came to be regarded as the only legitimate route to kingship.

As a foreign innovation the Davidic royal dynasty was at first without legitimation. It is now apparent that the poets at the Jerusalem court modeled their liturgies for the king's enthronement and other royal festivals upon the courtly literature of kingdoms in Egypt and Mesopotamia.[6] These liturgies, technically known as the Royal Psalms, are our best source of information concerning the ideology of sacral kingship in Southern Israel. To them we shall later return. The courtly style of these psalms, however, was at first no less alien to Yahwist tradition than dynastic kingship itself, and could not serve originally as its legitimation. A bridge between new and old, and legitimation of the former, was found in the idea of a covenant between Yahweh and David.

The covenant idea serves in the Old Testament as one of several schematic devices for interpreting Israel's history as a continuing engagement between Yahweh and his people. Any covenant with Yahweh, therefore, is a *historical* fact only in the sense that in actual use it was a way of viewing other historical data. The covenant schema itself, as distinguished from what it interprets, the Hebrews derived from the Hittites, possibly in the period of the Judges as early as the fourteenth century B.C. The interpretation of Abraham's dream of conquest and of the events at Sinai as corresponding to covenants initiated by Yahweh thus comprises comparatively late reinterpretations of events occurring in patriarchal and nomadic prehistory, memory of which had earlier been preserved in some other schema of explanation.[7] Unhappily, interpretive schemata invite ideological distortion, a danger to which Hebrew-Christian messianic interpretations of history are by no means immune.

Original legitimation of kingship in Israel rests upon an oracle of the court prophet, Nathan, announcing a covenant by which Yahweh has made David to be king. Mention of this covenant between Yahweh and his messiah is made in II Sam. 23:1-7, in what purports to be the last words of David. We can no longer be sure, however, as to the precise definitions of monarchy specified in the covenant as originally announced, for there is literary evidence that the oracle itself has been variously modified in transmission. We have three versions, found in II Sam., ch. 7, I Chron., ch. 17, and Ps. 89:20-37.

In its present form the account in II Samuel is the work of the Deuteronomist, from whose hand we have The Book of Judges, I and II Samuel, I and II Kings. Writing during the exile under the influence of the Deuteronomic reform movement, this unknown author has given us a theological reinterpretation of Israel's history. His minor thesis is that the very existence of the monarchy is the fundamental act of unfaith toward Yahweh responsible for the Babylonian captivity.

Fortunately, the Deuteronomist has incorporated into his account portions of documents from an earlier period, some of which are preserved largely unchanged except for occasional stylized interpolations of his own theological views. Among this material is the so-called Succession Document (II Sam. 6:23 to 20:26; I Kings, chs. 1 and 2), the work of an author who moved in Jerusalem court circles probably during the reign of Solomon, about four hundred years before the Deuteronomist compiled his "history." Recent research upon the Davidic covenant as it stands in the Succession Document (II Sam., ch. 7), discloses that even here is imbedded, in vs. 1-7, 11b, 16, 18-21, 25-29, a still more ancient formulation of Nathan's oracle — one, moreover, which bears striking resemblance to the Egyptian royal record.[8]

Examined in the light of the Egyptian court style upon which it is modeled, Nathan's oracle seems originally to have intended the legitimation of David's personal rule only. The pivotal expression is the term " house." The king's proposal to build a house for Yahweh (II Sam. 7:2) is countered by the announcement that Yahweh has built a house for David — apparently in the meaning of a secure relationship as Yahweh's son. The strikingly new thing for Israel in the oracle is the conception of the king as the son of God, an idea the sense of which we shall have to explore further.[9]

The revised oracle, as it appeared even in the ancient Succession Document, identifies the dynasty as the " house " built by Yahweh for David, thus legitimating the royal line as a whole. Of equal significance theologically, the revision announces the establishment of the monarchy *in perpetuity* as a fundamental expression of Yahweh's relation to Israel. " Your house and your kingdom shall be made sure for ever [*ad olam*] before me; your throne shall be established for ever." (II Sam. 7:16.)

The version of Nathan's oracle found in I Chron., ch. 17, is the work of the Chronicler, who has given us from the fourth century B.C. another theological reinterpretation of Israel's history, comprising the books of Chronicles, Ezra, and Nehemiah. His version of the oracle, like the whole of his writing, is fundamentally dependent upon the work of the Deuteronomist,[10] to which in this case it brings nothing new.

The oracle as it appears in Ps. 89:19-37 specifically subordinates the dynasty to the Sinaitic law, and yet makes clear that Yahweh's covenant with David is not conditioned by the perfect obedience of his successors.

I will not violate my covenant,
    or alter the word that went forth from my lips.
Once for all I have sworn by my holiness;
    I will not lie to David.
His line shall endure for ever,
    his throne as long as the sun before me.
Like the moon it shall be established for ever;
    it shall stand firm while the skies endure.

(Ps. 89:34-37.)

The relationship between this formulation of the oracle and that in II Sam., ch. 7, is much in dispute. The poetry of the psalm is commonly held to be an extensive elaboration of the prose of II Samuel. Yet by others it is argued that the prose version in the Succession Document is directly dependent upon the royal liturgies of the Jerusalem Temple, of which Ps. 89 is typical.[11] Hence it is possible, but by no means established, that Nathan first uttered in an actual enthronement ceremony his oracle announcing Yahew's covenant with King David.

It should be remembered, however, that the king in ancient Israel was also the Lord's messiah. The Davidic dynasty, therefore, was at once a theologically legitimated line of kings and a politically oriented messianic movement. The messianic aspect of the royal dynasty was expressly declared. In Ps. 132:17, for example, the poet has Yahweh say of Jerusalem, with obvious reference to the Davidic covenant, " There I will make a horn to sprout for David; I have prepared a lamp for my messiah." [12] Thus Nathan's oracle originally legitimated the reign of David only. Yet by a process of recurrent theological transformation, begun as early as Solomon's accession to the throne, it became the ideological foundation of messianic kingship as a going social institution. When the messianic establishment failed, the oracle became by the same process the historical source and legitimation of all subsequent messianic expectation — the wellspring of Hebrew-Christian messianism.[13]

HE IDEOLOGY OF HEBREW MESSIANIC KINGSHIP

ng the period of the Judges, conservative opposition to the monarchial movement rallied around the idea that in Israel no king was necessary, for Yahweh was king (I Sam. 8:7; 12:12; Judg. 8:23). Yet the use of this argument meant that already even conservative Yahwism was assimilating into its thought structure the alien ideology of kingship borrowed from its neighbors. Yahweh's sovereignty and his kingdom are imported ideas.

When monarchy was fully established, the kingship of Yahweh continued to serve, now as a concept both defining and limiting the political and cultic authority of the reigning king. Celebration of the sovereignty of Yahweh was the purpose of a regular festival in which processions of the people poured into the Temple to join in the liturgical acclamation of Yahweh's enthronement. Description of such a festival is preserved in Ps. 68:24-27. The enthronement psalms, central to the liturgies of these occasions, celebrate the character and extent of Yahweh's rule: The Lord reigns; let the earth rejoice and the peoples tremble. He is a great God, a great King above all gods. He sits enthroned in Zion upon the cherubim — enthroned over the flood and the powers of nature. He is a great King over all the earth. He reigns over the nations; he is exalted above all the peoples. Lover of justice, he comes to rule the earth and to judge the world with righteousness and the peoples with equity. [14] More specifically, Yahweh's rule is the basic fact in Israelite royalism, " For it is Yahweh who is really our shield; it is the Holy One of Israel who is really our king " (Ps. 89:18); [15] it is he who gives the glory of empire to his faithful (Ps. 149).

The way in which the kingship of Yahweh served ideologically to legitimate and limit the powers of the human king is best seen through the royal psalms — liturgical poems used in ceremonies whose central figure was the king.[16] Striking is the fact that in half the royal psalms " messiah " — in the meaning of

Yahweh's "anointed" — is used as an equivalent term for "king." [17] In this and other ways the king was reminded of his responsibility to Yahweh and of his dependence upon him.

The broad powers of the king derived from the idea that he was Yahweh's son. This radical innovation quite early found its way into the terms of the Davidic covenant. (Ps. 89:26-27; II Sam. 7:14.) It is dramatically expressed in words prescribed for the king in his coronation liturgy: "I will tell of the decree of the Lord: He said to me, 'You are my son, today I have begotten you'" (Ps. 2:7). Significantly, this filial relationship dates from the king's actual elevation to the throne. He is not begotten of God in the processes of his physical origin, but precisely in the event of his enthronement; [18] he is a son not by right of birth but by adoption. He is therefore not a god (cf. II Kings 5:7). Especially is he not Yahweh masquerading in the form of a man. He is emphatically and precisely a man who, in his royal functions and by divine appointment, is also Yahweh's son.

As the son of God, the king is also heir to the nations over whom Yahweh bears rule. "Ask of me, and I will make the nations your heritage, and the ends of the earth your possession. You shall break them with a rod of iron, and dash them in pieces like a potter's vessel." The implication follows that the nations doing obeisance to the king of Israel are really acknowledging the sovereignty of Yahweh. (Ps. 2:8, 9.) By rights, therefore, the king has dominion over the whole world, [19] for the throne upon which he sits he shares with Yahweh. (Ps. 101:1.) [20] Ideologically, therefore, messianic kingship in ancient Israel was political imperialism in theological form.

The rule of Yahweh and that of the king, however, were never regarded as identical. During the period of the monarchy, God's sovereign action in the affairs of Israel was unquestioned. All that happened was taken to be an expression of his will. However tangled the threads of meaning perceptible in the surface of actual events, his purpose was assumed to be their underlying and all-inclusive pattern. The sovereignty of Israel's

:ings over the nations, by contrast, depended upon a right rela-
:ion to Yahweh. His rule must exhibit the righteousness and
justice of God. Yet Yahweh's righteousness and justice were
themselves ambiguously conceived. On the one hand, they embraced his universal concern for the poor, the needy, the victim
of violence and oppression. Thus a prayer for the realization of
the king's dominion over the whole world stipulates as the
appropriate reason:

> For he delivers the needy when he calls,
>   the poor and him who has no helper.
> He has pity on the weak and the needy,
>   and saves the lives of the needy.
> From oppression and violence he redeems their life;
>   and precious is their blood in his sight.
>   (Ps. 72:12-14.)

On the other hand, the divine righteousness is specifically
Yahweh's faithfulness to Israel — his continuing fulfillment of
obligations inherent in a relation he himself has established with
her.[21] Thus we find in the Song of Deborah a very ancient reference to " Yahweh's righteous acts " (Judg. 5:11), in this case
a euphemism for Yahweh's role in Israel's wars of defense and
conquest. Messianic royalism located its inherent ideological
imperialism precisely in this traditional conception of divine
justice and righteousness (cf. Ps. 89:14, 24-39), and easily
concluded that victorious conquest itself validates and appropriately rewards the king's fidelity in his relation to Yahweh
(cf. Ps. 18:20-45).

In foreign policy, the messiah's chief role was leadership in
war (I Sam. 10:1), for which Yahweh himself trained his hand
(Ps. 18:34). From this there was but a short and tempting step
to the messianic pretension that the action of Israel's armies
was precisely the work of the Lord. (Ps. 18:39, 50; 21:8-12;
89:23-25.) In any case, David's successful conquest of Palestine fitted beautifully into the pattern of ideas surrounding the
throne. Later, when conflicts of interest arose between Israel

and foreign powers too strong to be conquered, the ideology of the cult could give no clear mandate for the realistic conduct of foreign policy. This embarrassment was heightened, as we shall see, by the fact that the prevailing customs in treaty-making violated the king's cultic obligations to Yahwism at home.

In domestic affairs, the role of the king was more sharply restrained by the traditions of desert Yahwism. Especially in Northern Israel, but so too in Judah, his claim to election and anointment by Yahweh set him apart to rule, but only as the first among his peers. Psalm 72 provides a virtual catalogue of the hopes invested by his subjects in their king. The psalm conveys as its broadest meaning the expectation that the king shall mediate those blessings of Yahweh indispensable to the welfare of the people as a whole. The first blessing besought for him, and through him for the people, is his endowment with the justice and righteousness of God. (Ps. 72:1-4.) The outcropping of divine righteousness in the life of the king and of his subjects was not a matter of obedience to minute details of inflexible law. Its exhibition was rather in conduct creatively responsive to relations existing or contracted between actual people.[22] Proper interpersonal relations, of course, were broadly defined and their breaches rigorously punished according to hallowed custom. Yet within the broad limits set by custom there was room for a wide variety of specific arrangements mutually acceptable to the parties concerned. This wide freedom to negotiate specifics invited the exploitation of the weak by the strong. The divine righteousness and justice of the king was at once the bulwark of sacred custom and the defense of the poor, the needy, the oppressed.

As a mediator between Yahweh and the people, however, the royal messiah himself stood not over but under the righteousness and justice of God. The monarch could be called into line by the prophet, for in his proper role the latter stood before Yahweh and the people as fully the king's equal. Classic illustration is found in Nathan's challenge to David concerning his affair with Bathsheba and his murder of her husband, Uriah (II Sam. 11:3-

39), and in Elijah's oracle against Ahab after the murder of
Naboth for possession of his vineyard (I Kings 21:1-19).
David's perception and acceptance of a single standard for the
king and his subjects, through this encounter with Nathan, is
one of the marks of his greatness.

The king was the medium as well through whom Yahweh
bestowed upon the people his blessings of material well-being.
(Ps. 72:3, 15-17.) Through him were expected the divine blessings of profitable trade, abundant harvest, and increase of the
population. By breach of sacral custom, of course, the king
could bring Yahweh's curse upon his subjects, and so upon himself, for the people were his royal possession. Thus when David
violated an ancient taboo by taking a military census, his prophet,
Gad, confronted him with an oracle giving him a choice of
three evils, one of which must befall Israel. Significantly, he
decided against the calamity of military reverses, preferring to
throw himself directly upon the wrath and mercy of God without the risk of human mediation (II Sam. 24:14).

We have mentioned the obligation of the king to preserve
inviolate the relations of the people one to another under Yahweh. After the time of Solomon, he had the further duty to
maintain and repair the Temple at Jerusalem. Aside from these
cultic functions, however, the monarch seems to have exercised
a priestly role, the character and importance of which is a
matter of continuing dispute.[23] Tradition has it that sacrifices
were offered by David (II Sam. 6:13; 24:25), by Solomon (I
Kings 3:4-5; 8:62-64; 9:25; 10:5), and even by Jereboam in
Israel proper after the division of the kingdom (I Kings 12:32).
David, moreover, had established his dynasty upon the ideological foundations stemming from the ancient priest-king,
Melchizedek, of Jerusalem. In one of the coronation liturgies,
the king is reminded of the Lord's oath to him: " You are a
priest for ever after the order of Melchizedek " (Ps. 110:4).

It is clear that the monarchy increasingly pictured itself as
a central and indispensable mediator of Yahweh's presence in
the life of the people. Yet the evidence by no means supports

the radical conclusion that the king, like his Babylonian and Egyptian counterparts, was " the supreme leader of the priesthood." [24] Likewise dubious is the thesis that the king of Judah in his priestly role took part annually in ritual combat and humiliation through which, as the suffering servant and humble messiah of Yahweh, he re-presented God's aboriginal victory over the powers of chaos and darkness.[25] Explicit references to sufferings of the Lord's messiah, as in Ps. 18:4 ff. and 89:38 ff., are most probably rooted in historical events rather than in ancient mythological ritual. Thus Ps. 89 in its present form, though it preserves material from the period of the monarchy, is most likely a lament over the catastrophe of the Babylonian exile. Moreover, despite reference to the king as in a special sense the servant of Yahweh (e.g., II Sam. 3:18; 7:5; I Kings 3:6 f.; Ps. 89:3, 20), there is in monarchial ideology no anticipation of the idea, found in Second Isaiah, that God appoints the sufferings of a blameless servant for healing the iniquity of the guilty (Isa., chs. 52; 53). In Ps. 18, the king presents himself as temporarily the innocent victim of suffering — a startling theological innovation in itself, but his vindication is a purely military victory. This worldly messianic royalism knew nothing of a suffering which was precisely a victory over the world.

We have mentioned an ideological handicap upon the king's treaty-making function. Ideological coexistence was frequently the substance of royal foreign policy. Hot war often, cold war otherwise, was long the party line of conservative Yahwism. Cultic purity, moreover, required every Israelite to acknowledge no god other than Yahweh. The king was especially bound to promote no other worship. Yet the provisions of important foreign alliances were customarily cemented by royal marriage. As one of his treaty obligations to the numerous wives he thus acquired for reasons of state, the king was expected to make provision at court for each to worship according to the rites of her native religion.

Pronounced condemnation of this practice is evident in the historicotheological work of the Deuteronomist, written after the fall of Judah. His retrospective censure itself reflects the earlier Deuteronomic reform movement originating in Israel proper under the reign of Josiah. Yet prophetic attack upon the custom goes back much farther. Ruthless opposition to foreign cult practices introduced by Jezebel, the Phoenician wife of Ahab, for example, contributed to the overthrow of the dynasty of Omri (II Kings 9:1-26) — a short-lived line which provided outstanding leadership on the throne of the Northern Kingdom. The direct agent of this particular coup was an army officer named Jehu; but in the background appears the fine hand of the prophet Elisha. After an emissary from the prophet had anointed Jehu and designated him the next king of Israel, the newly named messiah proceeded to murder the reigning king and all other living members of the Omri family in order the more quickly to launch his own dynasty.

Appropriate at this point is an examination of the ideological claim that the king is a charismatic person — that is, one directly under the influence of Yahweh's Spirit. The assimilation of messianic royalism into Hebrew life would have been incomplete without this idea; for the charismatic was a distinctive element in Yahwistic understanding of Israel's existence.[26] The claim of royal inspiration was reiterated during several phases of the monarchy, starting in the formative period. The Spirit of the Lord is said to have come mightily upon David from the day of his anointment forward. (I Sam. 16:13.) Tradition holds that upon occasion he prophesied, claiming divine inspiration for his words: " The Spirit of the Lord speaks by me, his word is upon my tongue " (II Sam. 23:2). God's endowment of Solomon for his reign is the subject of a detailed report. (I Kings 3:5-14.) Though in actual practice the king's conduct of political affairs was often divorced from any concern for the deeper meaning of his action, the divine inspiration of his decisions was proverbial (Prov. 16:10). Finally, toward the close of the monarchy — while Judah stood under the threat of Assyrian invasion — the prophet Isaiah recalled her king to a charismatic understanding of his office (Isa. 11:1-5)

Still, a certain ambiguity in Israel's attitude toward the charismatic is early evident. Our earliest accounts of her life under the Judges make clear, for example, that the ecstatic cult hero is jeopardized by the burden of the divine charisma he bears. He may fritter it away, and so destroy himself along with the enemies of his people, as in the case of Samson (Judg. 16:30); or it may be taken from him and given to another, as in the case of Saul (I Sam. 16:13-14).[27] The adoption of messianic kingship may be viewed, then, as an effort to prolong and stabilize charismatic leadership through sacred institution.

The very idea of an institutionalized charisma, however, involves a fundamental tension between the censorious and re-creative spontaneity of the inspired individual, on the one hand, and the predictable customs, procedures, and expectations that soon become associated with his public office, on the other. This tension, we might add parenthetically, characterizes Hebrew-Christian self-understanding from the rise of the monarchy onward.

From the very beginning, the southern tribes were more inclined than the northern to contain and curtail the charismatic by institutional forms. In Judah, for example, restriction of royal succession to the male descendents in David's line was accepted as an arrangement initiated by Yahweh himself through his covenant with David. In Northern Israel, where no such restriction applied, the divine Spirit would seem to have had greater freedom to operate. That the will of the people, or of the prophet, or of the court bureaucracy would be more responsive than genetics to the will of God proved, nevertheless, to be an unwarranted assumption. Moreover, the minimal customs developed in Northern Israel for determining access to the throne turned out to be readily manipulable for partisan interests. Hence, even in the case of Israel proper, to speak of royal succession as charismatic is repeatedly to employ a pretentious euphemism for unstable government, political intrigue, and civil war.

Ordinarily not the king but the prophet was the preeminent

charismatic person in ancient Israel. David was an exception. His political genius and his rapid expansion of the empire seemed to accredit his claim to special knowledge of Yahweh's intention. Royal leadership alone, however inspired, could never have raised Israel, whether united or divided, to her status as a third-rate political power. Her rise would have been impossible apart from a lull in the struggle among her great neighbors for world dominion. When that lull was over the destiny of the Hebrew monarchies stood at the disposal of the Assyrian and neo-Babylonian empires. The royal governments of the two Hebrew kingdoms in Judah and Israel proper each confronted the menace of foreign power with the conviction of its own manifest destiny to rule the nations. In terms of the ideology of messianic kingship, the subjection of Yahweh's people to a non-Hebrew power was conceivable only upon the assumption of ethnic guilt. Even the Hebrew prophetic movement split over the meaning of the Assyrian and Babylonian threat to the people of Yahweh's choosing. Those prophets who envisioned eventual Hebrew dominance of political history were the victims of Hebrew messianic pretensions. On the other hand, even those prophets who renounced the imperialist dream were yet themselves the victims of royalist ideology to the extent that they found the impending political catastrophe wholly intelligible in terms of Yahweh's wrath against his people. The impact of Hebrew prophecy upon messianic royalism as an actual political institution, however, and the new shape given by prophecy to messianic expectation when the imminent failure of the monarchies became visible must engage our attention in a later chapter.

Sufficient for the moment is the observation that institutional perspectives tended to distort or to block altogether the charismatic vision of the ruling kings. From the early days of the monarchy the king's role in ordinary affairs of state tended to be secularized. Recruitment of manpower for the army and civilian labor forces, logistics, fortification, taxation, and public works were treated increasingly as technical matters. Momentous decisions, especially in foreign policy, were more and more shaped by a stereotyped image of the king's office rather than by innovative inspiration.

THE END OF HEBREW MONARCHY

By 732 B.C., Assyria had conquered coastal Palestine and had left Judah, a reduced Israel, and a number of their small neighbors in control of their internal affairs on the condition of the annual payment of tribute. In 721 B.C., Hoshea, the king of Israel, refused tribute and attempted an alliance with Egypt against Assyria. Sargon II retaliated immediately. He crushed Samaria, the capital city, removed Hoshea to prison, scattered his subjects among the outlying provinces of the Assyrian empire, and resettled the land with exiles from a variety of subjugated peoples. (II Kings 17:4-6, 24.) So ended messianic kingship in Northern Israel.

In 701 B.C., Judah would have suffered the same fate at Assyrian hands had it not been for Sennacherib's reluctance to destroy the country. He forced the acknowledgment of his rule and the resumption of tribute by destroying the fortifications of all Judean cities except Jerusalem, which he saved in exchange for a special payment of heavy tribute. (II Kings 18:13-16.) While Assyria was strong Judah remained compliant. Except for a single abortive revolt, Manasseh kept his people ruthlessly in line. Their nationalism he undercut by introducing the worship of foreign gods.

When Assyria's rapid disintegration set in, Manasseh's son, Josiah, repudiated the foreign cults, first in Judah and then as far north as Galilee, thereby announcing his political control over two Assyrian provinces and stirring memories of David's claim to a united Israel. (II Chron. 34:3-7.) His final break with Assyria was also under the guise of a religious act. In 622 B.C., at about the time Babylon threw off the Assyrian yoke, Josiah instituted a sweeping revival of Yahwism on the basis of an ancient Book of the Law uncovered in the course of repairing the Temple. He prohibited public worship at alien shrines and ordered the systematic desecration of their altars. He achieved for the first time a worship of Yahweh centralized in Jerusalem, where syncretistic tendencies could be more easily controlled. For these measures, his fame was enduring. (II Kings 23:25.)

Josiah lost his life in battle at the pass of Megiddo, a historic bottleneck in transportation between Egypt and Asia Minor. Here his troops also suffered defeat, yet they managed to prevent Neco's Egyptian army from joining with Assyrian forces to crush the rising power of Babylon. Judah's subsequent vassalage to Egypt was brief. At the Battle of Carchemish in 605 B.C., Babylon routed Egypt's forces and established *de facto* control over the petty kingdoms of Palestine. Judean foreign policy thus produced in the end no more than the exchange of the Assyrian for the Babylonian yoke.

Three years after Carchemish, Jehoiakim of Judah revolted. Retaliation came in March of 597 B.C., when Nebuchadnezzar besieged Jerusalem and carried away into Babylonian captivity the newly crowned Jehoachin and his more prominent subjects. Nebuchadnezzar placed upon Judah's throne Jehoachin's uncle, Zedekiah, who proved to be a rebellious puppet. Finally, his patience exhausted, the emperor obliterated the towns of Judah and in 587 B.C. destroyed Jerusalem and the Temple. Zedekiah's sons were slain before his eyes; he was then blinded and taken with most of the remaining populace into exile. So ended messianic royalism as an effective political force in Judah.

HEBREW MONARCHY IN RETROSPECT

A striking feature of Hebrew messianic kingship was the wide disparity between its ideology and its actual performance. At first glance, this apparent loss of touch with political reality would seem to have an adequate explanation in the fact that the Hebrews borrowed from the great world powers not only the techniques of monarchial government but also the propaganda rationalizing imperial dominion. The minstrels at the Jerusalem court quite evidently imitated the poet courtiers of Egypt and Mesopotamia when they called their king the son of Yahweh; his seat, Yahweh's throne; his claim to world empire, divine right; his power in subjugating foreign peoples, divine might; his domestic rule, an exhibition of the universal dominion, justice, and blessing of Yahweh. Of course such description, transferred to the king of tiny Judah, only made his modest power appear the smaller.

Yet we miss the underlying seriousness in the language of the royal psalms if we suppose that in this borrowing the Hebrew minstrel intended merely to flatter his king or, in poetic hyperbole, to express good wishes for his reign. The adoption of this language gave new expression to something already deeply ingrained in Hebraic understanding of Yahweh's relation to his chosen people.

The ideas commonly associated with Yahweh's messiah and his empire have appropriately been called " prophetic exegeses of Nathan's prophecy " concerning David.[28] That is to say, the first intention of the language is theological; its political content is consequent and incidental. In terms of Hebrew thought, it follows that a fundamental clash between messianic propaganda and the actual history of the monarchy, insofar as it signifies bad thinking, requires first of all a reconstruction of prophetic theology. Further, the taint of ideological distortion in Hebrew royalism is appropriately to be sought in theologies of history rather than in political ideology as such.

Yet precisely because Hebrew messianic royalism is characteristically a theology of *history,* the events of 721 and 587 B.C. provide clues to its inherent theological distortions. According to the prevailing interpretations of Nathan's prophecy, the future of David's line and with it the political existence of Judah were perpetually assured. (II Sam. 7:13, 16.) That is to say, Hebrew messianism tended to conceive of the monarchy as a continuously dependable expression within history of

Yahweh's faithfulness to his chosen people. For in the covenant Yahweh himself had promised a lamp in Jerusalem for David and his sons forever. (I Kings 11:36; 15:4; II Chron. 21:7; Ps. 132:17.) The efforts of certain of the prophets themselves in the late stages of the monarchy to correct this prophetic fallacy will later engage our attention.

The distressing clash between prevailing prophetic expectation and the actual history of kingship receives in Ps. 89 a startling theological explanation: Yahweh has gone back on his word. He has canceled a covenant that he himself had sworn unconditionally to keep forever. (Ps. 89:30-39.) The psalmist spells out Yahweh's renunciation in painful imagery that applies to the whole messianic dynasty no less than to its living and deposed representative.

> But now thou hast cast off and rejected,
>   thou art full of wrath against thy messiah.
> Thou hast renounced the covenant with thy servant;
>   thou hast defiled his crown in the dust.
> Thou hast breached all his walls;
>   thou hast laid his strongholds in ruins.
> All that pass by despoil him;
>   he has become the scorn of his neighbors.
> Thou hast exalted the right hand of his foes;
>   thou hast made all his enemies rejoice.
> Yea, thou hast turned back the edge of his sword,
>   and thou hast not made him stand in battle.
> Thou hast removed the scepter from his hand,
>   and cast his throne to the ground.
> Thou hast cut short the days of his youth;
>   thou hast covered him with shame.
>   (Ps. 89:38-45.)

For the psalmist, however, the divine wrath is not without its reason; the divine will still makes Judah's past intelligible, her future hopeful. In response to national tragedy, therefore, he places upon the lips of his king a trusting appeal to the very faithfulness of Yahweh:

> Lord, where is thy steadfast love of old,
>> which by thy faithfulness thou didst swear to David?
> Remember, O Lord, how thy servant is scorned;
>> how I bear in my bosom the insults of the peoples,
> with which thy enemies taunt, O Lord,
>> with which they mock the footsteps of thy messiah.
>>> (Ps. 89:49-51.)

The most accurate portrayal of conditions in Judah during the exile is found in the five short poems which together comprise the book of Lamentations. Amid the description of famine, the confession of guilt, and the remembrance of the ravaging invaders is this despairing admission that hope was misplaced in the king:

> The breath of our nostrils, the Lord's messiah,
>> was taken in their pits,
> he of whom we said, " Under his shadow
>> we shall live among the nations."
>>> (Lam. 4:20.)

Yet here is expressed the confidence that Yahweh soon is ending his punishment of Judah's iniquity and will keep her in exile no longer.

Agonizing theological reappraisal of the monarchy found expression not only in prophecy and psalmody but also in what we might call theistic saga — that characteristically Hebraic narrative form in which the author reconstructs the past around his understanding of what Yahweh was doing in and through the events recounted. The two authors, one known as the Deuteronomist, the other as the Chronicler, have each dealt with the monarchy in such a saga. Though separated by only a short time span, their two works come actually from two different eras. The Chronicler, writing after the exiles had returned to Jerusalem with permission from Cyrus to rebuild the Temple, records the labors of reconstruction. His appreciation of the monarchy indirectly foreshadows a messianism that finds its distinctive expression in liturgical rather than political action. Of that, more will be said later. The Deuteronomist by contrast, though writing in the suspended time of the exile, belongs still to the previous age.

We have mentioned already the Deuteronomist's low opinion of the monarchy. His critical attitude, however, is not entirely negative. Clearly, he prefers the amphictyony rather than the kingdom, spontaneous rather than dynastic leadership, as the ideal form of Hebrew existence. Yet Yahweh himself has acceded to the people's demand for a king. Let kings be judged then by Yahweh's expectations. The Deuteronomist finds his empirical standard for royal conduct in David. Solomon is measured against his father and found wanting: " His heart was not wholly true to the Lord his God, as was the heart of David his father," for he yielded to the enticement of his foreign wives to worship their alien gods (I Kings 11:4 f.). In reprisal for Solomon's defection, Yahweh is pictured as wresting from his heirs the ten northern tribes of the Kingdom and giving them to Jeroboam. To the latter, Yahweh promises through the prophet Ahijah: " If you will hearken to all that I command you, and will walk in my ways, and do what is right in my eyes by keeping my statutes and my commandments, as David my servant did," then your reign and that of your dynasty will be established over Israel (vs. 38 ff.). Later, through the same prophet, Yahweh pronounces judgment upon Jeroboam's performance: " You have not been like my servant David, who kept my commandments, and followed me with all his heart, doing only that which was right in my eyes, but you have done evil above all that were before you." For his defections, Jeroboam's line is condemned to utter annihilation. (I Kings 14:8 ff.) In these and repeated instances, the Deuteronomist compares the successive kings of Judah and Israel with the perfect David; he finds Josiah to be the only one who really stands up to his model (II Kings 22:2). " Before him there was no king like him, who turned to the Lord with all his heart and with all his soul and with all his might, according to all the law of Moses; nor did any like him arise after him." (II Kings 23:25.)

MESSIANIC KINGSHIP IN ANCIENT ISRAEL   39

We note several striking features in the theology of history which underlies this critique of Hebrew kingship.[29] First of all, he pushes the ideology of messianic kingship a step farther than the foreign models from which it originally derives. He supposes that the destiny of the Hebrew people is determined by decisions made for or against Yahweh in the heart of the king. This novel elevation of the king's role reverses the theological assumptions implicit in his description of Hebrew life under the Judges. Military reversals in that period are explained as Yahweh's reprisal upon the sins of the whole people. (Judg. 2:11-15; 3:7-8; 4:1-2; 6:1; 10:10; 13:1; I Sam. 7:6; etc.) The catastrophes befalling Israel and Judah, by contrast, are basically understood as divine visitations upon the sins of the people committed in the person of their kings.

In the second place, the kings of Judah and Israel are measured against an idealized David. The Deuteronomist achieves his portrait of a David perfect in all his relations to Yahweh by drastic retouching of the picture left to him by the author of the Succession Document. His preservation of the original unretouched sketch of his hero within his own work is astonishing. Only once does he recall the waywardness of David's own heart, and then in a casual reference to " the matter of Uriah the Hittite " (I Kings 15:5).

In the third place, the Deuteronomist interprets the monarchy as a prolongation of Hebrew salvation history. Before his time, the ideology of salvation history encompassed Yahweh's covenant with Abraham, promising him the land, the election of Israel, the sojourn in Egypt and the exodus under Moses, the covenant at Sinai with the deliverance of the Law, and concluded with the conquest of Canaan. The ideology of kingship comprised an independent literature. Thus Isaiah interprets life in Judah in the light of the Davidic covenant with no reference to the older covenant traditions. The book of Deuteronomy, on the other hand, though written during the period of the monarchy, looks back with longing to the days of the Yahwistic war cult under Moses, makes no mention of David or Zion, and scarcely acknowledges the existence of kings among the Hebrews. (Deut. 17:14-20.) The Deuteronomist's fusion of the two traditions in a single literary work constitutes a decided innovation. The novelty is not lessened by the fact that the elements of the fusion lay close together in the practice of the cult from the time that David brought the Ark to Jerusalem.

The full assimilation of monarchial ideology into conservative Hebrew self-understanding is clearly evident in the address that the Deuteronomist places upon the lips of Solomon on the occasion of the dedication of the Temple. Here Yahweh's covenant with David and his covenant with the patriarchs at Sinai are linked in a single train of thought. (I Kings 8:18-21.) The succeeding prayer of dedication opens with an appeal to Yahweh for confirmation of his covenant with David and closes with mention of the election of Israel, announced by Moses at the time of the exodus from Egypt. (Vs. 22-53.)

For the Deuteronomist, the wrath and mercy of Yahweh alone make intelligible the history of Hebrew monarchy — a wrath and mercy shaped by the ancient and continuing covenant relation between him and his people. The devastations of Israel and Judah are seen as resulting from the guilt of broken covenants. Destruction would have occurred much earlier had Yahweh not restrained his wrath in remembrance of his promises to Abraham, Isaac, and Jacob (II Kings 13:23) and to David (II Kings 8:19). By thus integrating messianic royalism into the older patterns of Hebraic thought, the Deuteronomist reclaimed the history of the monarchy from purely secular chronicle. He also reminded his people that their ultimate hope was in neither judges nor kings, but in Yahweh alone.

Appropriately, the theological test applied in this critique was the king's obedience to the Law of Yahweh. Yet Torah in his meaning was more than a codification of sacred commandment. It embraced basically an obligation to respond to the whole of Yahweh's dynamic activity in Hebrew history. So far as the king was concerned, the divine Law called for ultimate dependence upon nothing purely historical. He must ultimately seek

the well-being of his people neither in the powers of nature nor in foreign alliances, nor yet in his own fortifications and chariots of war. In his policies, domestic and foreign, he is dealing in the last analysis with Yahweh alone, who is the enemy of the gods and the only God there is.

If the cardinal virtue of the king is faithful obedience to Torah, conceived as the dynamic expression of Yahweh's presence in nature and history, his cardinal sin is idolatry. The Deuteronomist's interpretation of history is a rigorous exegesis of the first two of the Ten Sinaitic Commandments. Curiously enough, in spite of national catastrophe, he never perceived as idolatrous the messianic pretension that the Davidic dynasty stands above the ravages of time.

In the fourth place, the Deuteronomist thinks of world history as centering continuously in the Hebrew people. The election of Israel means, for him, that no other ethnic group can have under Yahweh a destiny coordinate with that of the Hebrews. Even in the terror of 721 and 587 B.C., he sees the other nations simply as unwitting instruments in Yahweh's dealings with Israel and Judah. Admirable for the very strength of its humanity is the courage to believe that the people of conquered and fragmented Judah — starving and defenseless in their homeland, bearing the yoke of slavery in Babylon — still had a place in the sun. Distortion is apparent, however, in the further conviction that in their placement in history the Hebrews are favored above all others. This distortion exhibits at once the genius and the weakness of Hebraic thought. The insight that purpose, value, guilt, and meaning are located in the unrepeatable history of persons and peoples is an abiding contribution to ethics and theology. The insight itself, though, is violated when those who have perceived its truth suppose that they can substitute themselves for the truth they have seen and heard as the organizing power in the existence of other groups. The Deuteronomist's adherence to the theological delusion that the parochial affairs of one obscure ethnic complex make intelligible the whole of human existence is remarkable only for its persistence against extraordinary pressure from historical facts.

The pressure of fact against theological schematization is evident as well as in the internal affairs of the Davidic dynasty. The chief villain in the royal succession was Manasseh. So infamous were his idolatries and his tyrannies, according to our author, that Yahweh announced through the prophets his resolve to work out upon Judah the destruction he had already wrought upon Israel. (II Kings 21:10 ff.) Intervening between Manasseh and the destruction of Jerusalem, however, was the reign of Josiah, who " did what was right in the eyes of the Lord, and walked in all the way of David his father, and he did not turn aside to the right hand or to the left " (II Kings 22:2). To him the Deuteronomist gives unstinting praise for his vigorous implementation of the reforms called for in the Deuteronomic theological revival. How explain, then, the fall of Jerusalem so shortly after Josiah's death? His answer is that even Josiah's fidelity could not turn aside the fierceness of Yahweh's wrath. There is a hiatus, then, between the sequence of actual events and the logic of the divine purpose expressed through it.

In the fifth place, the Deuteronomist carries through his critique of the kings on the assumption that the divine power takes in monarchial history the form of the word of Yahweh as spoken by the true prophet. This assumption is in marked contrast to that which underlies his account of tribal life under the Judges; he supposes that during that period Yahweh's presence was characteristically manifested in the charisma of the military hero rather than that of the prophet.

To show that the spirit of prophecy is the moving force of history in the time of the monarchy, he repeatedly cites prophetic predictions which have come true. A number of these involve an element of the miraculous: for example, the series of miracles performed by Elijah during his contest with Ahab and the prophets of Baal (I Kings, chs. 17; 18); Ahab's death in the battle of Ramoth-gilead, miraculously fulfilling predictions made by the prophets Elijah and Micaiah (I Kings 21:17-19;

22:19 ff.). A great many prophetic predictions, especially those relative to the monarchy, were fulfilled, however, through the ordinary dynamics of interpersonal and international relations. This fact calls for a closer examination of the ties between Hebrew prophets and Hebrew kings.

Chapter II

Hebrew Prophecy and Messianic Kingship

Monarchy took deeper root in Hebrew life than the prophet Samuel intended when he anointed first Saul and later David to be king over Israel. Bald military success, however, does not of itself explain David's achievement in converting a voluntary amphictyonic militia into a royal army, manned by conscription and supported by sometimes oppressive taxes. Likewise indispensable was the sort of legitimation provided by the oracle of Yahweh pronounced by Nathan the prophet. From the early years of the tenth century B.C., when the Davidic monarchy was accepted by all Hebrew tribes, until the middle of the ninth century, when Jehu succeeded Joram, Hebrew prophets, besides legitimating at their discretion the exercise of *de facto* royal power, often themselves made and unmade both kings and dynasties in Israel.

Thus Nathan had more than a ceremonial role in the anointing of Solomon as king; he played as well a decisive part in the palace politics which determined that Solomon, not Adonijah, would succeed David to the throne. (Cf. I Kings 1:5-48.)

While Solomon was still alive, the prophet Ahijah delivered an oracle in which, first, he sanctioned, before the fact, the secession of the ten northern tribes from the United Kingdom upon Solomon's death; and second, he designated an official of Solomon's court, Jeroboam, and his heirs in perpetuity as the legitimate claimants to the throne of Northern Israel — provided they walked in the ways of Yahweh as had David. (I Kings

11:29-38.) Solomon recognized in this action the creation of a deadly rival for his throne. His subsequent efforts to destroy Jeroboam were thwarted by the latter's finding political asylum in Egypt until Solomon's death from natural causes.

After Jeroboam's accession to the throne of Northern Israel, the same Ahijah laid upon him a curse for his failure to measure up to the prophet's Yahwist standards. (I Kings 14:10-14.) Under the aegis of this prophetic malediction, Baasha subsequently wiped out by regicide and murder the whole of Jeroboam's line. (I Kings 15:27-29.) Baasha evidently found prophetic legitimation for his own rise to power (I Kings 16:2); but he was soon accursed by the prophet Jehu for not measuring up (vs. 1-4). Thus by prophetic sanction Baasha's heirs received at the hands of Zimri the extermination that Baasha had himself measured out to Jeroboam's line. (Vs. 8-13.)

Zimri reigned for only seven days. Lacking prophetic legitimation, he was fair game for a military coup. When he saw that his fortress city was taken by troops under Omri, commander of the army, he retreated to the citadel of his palace and burned the whole structure over his head. (Vs. 15-18.)

Shortly before his death, Elijah seems to have divulged plans to anoint Hazael and Jehu for royal succession respectively in Syria and Israel. (Cf. I Kings 19:15-16.) Just what he had in mind in the first instance is no longer clear. In Jehu he quite obviously discerned an instrument capable of overthrowing the dynasty of Omri, all of whom were despised by the Yahwistic prophets, Ahab most especially. The final explosion of Elijah's wrath was set off by Ahab's connivance with Jezebel, his queen, in the murder of Naboth for possession of the latter's vineyard. The prophet died, however, before he could complete his arrangements for the *coup d'état*. To Elisha, therefore, fell the task of implementing Elijah's promise to wipe out every male in Ahab's line. (Cf. I Kings 21:20-24.)

Elisha first carried out the anointment of Hazael, conniving thereby at the murder of Benhadad, reigning king of Syria. (II Kings 8:7-15.) He next sent a prophetic emissary to Jehu, a commander in the royal army, at that time deployed for defense of the border against Syria. Elisha's deputy apparently had instructions to anoint Jehu king for the explicit purpose of destroying Ahab's line. (II Kings 9:1-10.) A later historian even speaks of Jehu as the one " whom the Lord had anointed to destroy the house of Ahab " (II Chron. 22:7). Jehu obliged with the murder, first, of King Joram, next, of the queen mother Jezebel, and finally, of seventy princes. (II Kings 9:14 to 10:17.)

Elisha's designation of Jehu as the king of Israel next after Joram seems to have marked a turn in the relationship between prophecy and the throne. During the prior 150 years, from the anointing of David around 1000 until the ascension of Jehu in 845-844 B.C., the prophets virtually controlled royal succession, first in the United Kingdom, and later in Northern Israel. Beyond the time of the Jehu insurrection we have no further evidence of the making and destroying of royal dynasties by prophetic oracle. Yet as late as the fifth century B.C., Nehemiah seems still to assume that accession to the throne is properly legitimated only by prophetic oracle. (Neh. 6:6 f.)

During the same one and one half centuries, the relationship between prophet and king ranged from close cooperation (cf. I Kings 20:13 f.; II Kings 3:14 f.) all the way to opposition (I Kings 22:8 f.) and implacable enmity. We have seen how the prophet's limited but very decisive power to designate kings and legitimate insurrection could embarrass and sometimes destroy a king. On the other hand, the king's power, for just cause, to decree the death of his subjects gravely menaced the prophet who dared oppose royal policy. Thus Ahab and Elijah were confessed enemies (I Kings 21:20 ff.); Jezebel, Ahab's queen, openly vowed to destroy the prophet (I Kings 19:2). Jehoiakim actually extradited from Egypt the prophet Uriah, son of Shemaiah, and put him to the sword for prophesying against Jerusalem and Judah. (Jer. 26:20 ff.) If prophets after Elisha no longer determined royal succession, they still exercised a political influence no monarch could safely ignore. The prophet, moreover, whose message was unpopular continued to speak his oracle at some risk to his neck. As late as the Babylonian invasion of Judah, Jeremiah's activity twice brought him to a close brush with death at the hands of the princes in Zedekiah's court.

The menace of Assyria and later of Babylon, however, effected in the character of Hebrew prophecy and in the relation of prophets to the king a greater change than any wrought by the infighting of Hebrew domestic politics. Before the black cloud of these tremendous imperialist systems, prophets of the eighth and later centuries became convinced that Yahweh willed the suspension of Hebrew statehood in punishment for the disloyalty and injustices of his people. The role of prophecy in the dissolution of the monarchy varied, of course, with the individual prophet and with the shifting international situation. Of greater theological significance, however, is the fact that the foundering of the state disclosed in prophecy itself theological fallacies analogous to the illusions that persistently flawed the ideology of messianic kingship. Because of the underlying kinship between prophetic and monarchic theologies of history, a brief examination of the prophetic critique of the throne can be expected not only to illumine the historical impasse of Hebrew monarchy but also to shed some light upon the fact that prophecy in its classical form did not long survive the loss of Hebrew political independence.

PROPHETIC ORACLES ON THE DESTRUCTION OF THE HEBREW STATE

Amos. The Judean herdsman, Amos, was moved by domestic corruption and the mounting flood of Assyrian imperialism abroad to prophesy against Jeroboam II (786–746 B.C.) and the Northern Kingdom: " Jeroboam shall die by the sword, and Israel must go into exile away from his land " (Amos 7:11). He delivered his first oracles in Samaria, the capital city, and his last at the king's chapel in Bethel.

Amaziah, the king's chaplain at Bethel, there charged the

prophet with conspiracy and delivered a royal edict ordering his return to Judah and forbidding his ever again prophesying at the shrine. Amos answered the charge of conspiracy by denying any connection with the guilds in which the prophets were professionally trained in the gentle arts of induced ecstasy and insurrection. No professional prophet he, but simply a shepherd whom Yahweh had taken from following his flock to deliver a message of doom upon Israel. He made it clear that Amaziah himself and his wife would be among those taken by Assyria into exile. (Amos 7:10-17.) Amos, nevertheless, retired to his native Tekoa in Judah. There he reduced his oracles to writing and added to them accounts of visions in which he elaborated predictions of destruction unfulfilled until Samaria fell in 721 B.C., a generation later.

Internal evidence suggests that the book bearing his name took its present shape after the Babylonian destruction of Jerusalem in 587 B.C. The main features of his message, however, are clearly evident in those portions of the book generally regarded as his authentic work. Securely attributed to him are the oracles of chs. 1 to 6 and of ch. 8:4-14, excepting, possibly, those to Tyre, Edom, Judah, and the Philistines, together with most of the visions recorded in chs. 7 to 9.

Yahweh's sovereignty over all peoples resounds as a minor theme in his thought. His oracles to the nations are addressed to Syria, Ammon, and Moab as well as to Israel. If Amos 9:7 was written by him, he suggests that Israel is no better than any other nation in Yahweh's eyes: " ' Are you not like the Ethiopians to me, O people of Israel? ' says the Lord. ' Did I not bring up Israel from the land of Egypt, and the Philistines from Caphtor and the Syrians from Kir? ' "

This universalism is aborted, however, by the tacit assumption, first, that messianic royalism is the ultimate order of human existence, and second, that though all nations are equal before Yahweh, Israel is somehow more equal than others. The prophet predicts punishment, indeed, but the very demands of retributive justice are a measure of Israel's favored position with God:

" You only have I known of all the families of the earth; therefore I will punish you for all your iniquities " (Amos 3:2).

The dominant structure of his thought remained, therefore,
an application of monarchial theology suited to the historical
situation in which Assyrian imperialism was decisively significant. The new note in his theology is his prediction that Yahweh's action will be against Israel, not for her. He foresees a
future in which Jacob is delivered to his enemies, not from them.
If it is granted that Amos was the author of ch. 5:6, 15, his
hope for Israel's future rested wholly upon the divine mercy,
and envisioned benefits of an entirely secular sort: " Hate evil,
and love good, and establish justice in the gate; it may be that
the Lord, the God of hosts, will be gracious to the remnant of
Joseph."

Real and damaging enough are the domestic inequities, the
fraudulent piety, and the national pride of which the prophet
complains. With scorching tongue he excoriates the rich of
Israel, especially the wealthy matrons (" cows of Bashan "),
for their oppression of the poor, for their greed and conspicuous
consumption, for their bribes and perversions of justice at law.
(Amos 2:6-8; 5:11-12; 6:11-14.) He execrates the noise of
solemn assemblies celebrating in ceremonious liturgy a divine
justice daily denied at court, at law, in commerce and industry.
(Ch. 5:21-24.) He scorns the nation's pride in Jeroboam's conquest of Damascus and his restoration of the Davidic boundaries
between Israel and Syria. (Ch. 6:8.) Yet in all this his thought
follows basically the ideology of messianic kingship. Thus he
sees world events as an enlarged projection of Israel's domestic
affair with Yahweh. In this perspective, Israel's foreseeable
decline as a power among nations could only mean her guilt
before God.

Hosea. The prophetic work of Hosea ended near the conclusion of the Syro-Ephraimitic War, 735–734 B.C. The Assyrian invasion of Israel was then still in the future. Samaria, the
capital city, fell in 721 B.C.

Hosea takes the marriage relation between himself and Gomer as a personal analogue of Yahweh's relation to Israel. This theme alone makes of his prophetic work a coherent whole. His love for Gomer, her breach of their marriage covenant through harlotry, his purchase of her freedom and restoration of their marriage out of love and covenant loyalty (*hesedh*) to her: all this provides analogies for the prophet's estimate of the current historical scene and for his understanding of the impending fall of Israel before Assyria.[1]

As between Gomer and the prophet, so between Israel and Yahweh there exists a harlotrous breach of covenant loyalty. In Israel's case, disloyalty takes both a religious and a political form. (Cf. Hos. 5:1-4; 10:8-10.)

The political aspects of this harlotry, in his view, revolve around the throne. At first reading, he seems to take the very existence of messianic kingship as disloyalty to Yahweh. In any case, he envisions the impending Assyrian storm as Yahweh's punishment for a defect inherent in the monarchy from its founding. " From the days of Gibeah [Saul's home], you have sinned, O Israel " (Hos. 10:9); in Gilgal (where Saul was crowned) " I began to hate them " (ch. 9:15).

On second reading, his attack upon royalism may be taken, possibly, as directed not so much against political messianism as such, but against its attempt to manipulate events as if kings were gods. He excoriates Jehu, not because he is a king by prophetic anointment, but because he mounted the throne by assassinating Ahab on the plain of Jezreel (Hos. 1:4), and by subsequently obliterating Ahab's line. He attacks a monarchy perpetuated solely by political intrigue and assassination. (Ch. 7:5-7.) He voices as Yahweh's complaint: " They made kings, but not through me. They set up princes, but without my knowledge " (ch. 8:4).

Similarly, his critique of the royal defense policy is capable alike of moderate or of extreme interpretation. Possibly his protest against Israel's trust in her chariots and the size of her army (Hos. 10:13) constitutes no theological objection to armament in principle. He may intend, rather, to challenge an underlying assumption that history is finally determined by military might.

Less ambiguous is his castigation of royal diplomacy: " Like a dove, silly and without sense, calling to Egypt, going to Assyria " (Hos. 7:11). He objects to payment of tribute (chs. 12:1; 8:10) and repudiates entangling foreign alliances (chs. 5:13-14; 7:8-9). He speaks no word as to the positive political content of a foreign policy soundly grounded in the covenant relation between Israel and Yahweh. His adverse criticisms of foreign diplomacy are aimed, not at the details of specific political arrangements, but at all international treaties. Foreign alliances as such constitute for him a disloyalty to Yahweh, in part because the protocol of divine kingship required the contracting parties to give mutual recognition to their respective deities. He strongly opposed the attendant introduction into Israel of foreign, and often debasing, cult practices. Yet basically his objection rests upon a theology of history that is the prophetic counterpart of the ideology of messianic kingship itself. Clearly, he regards the charismatic prophet as the effective agent of the divine purpose (ch. 12:13) and prophetic prediction as the basic instrumentality through which Yahweh operates within history (ch. 6:5). He calls for a foreign policy that involves a theological stance rather than political action: In every crisis depend upon Yahweh to pass a miracle through the mouth of his prophet. No other diplomacy or defense is needed.

Yahweh's response to Israel's disloyalty is quite clear to Hosea. The covenant is repudiated from God's side: " You are not my people and I am not your God " (Hos. 1:9). He has deserted them (ch. 5:6) and will love them no more (ch. 9:15). Yahweh has become to Israel like a moth, like dry rot (ch. 5:12), like a lion or a leopard (ch. 13:7). Like a bear robbed of her cubs, he will fall upon them to rend and devour. (V. 8.)

The Lord himself will recompense her double harlotry. Her altars and pillars will be wiped out (Hos. 10:2), her hilltop shrines destroyed (v. 8), her fertility symbol smashed (ch. 8:5) or hauled off to Assyria (ch. 10:6). The mirth of her religiosity, her feasts, her new moons, her sabbaths, and her appointed feasts will all be ended (ch. 2:11), and she shall be punished for her worship of Baal (v. 13). "A vulture is over the house of the Lord, because they have broken my covenant." (Ch. 8:1.) Israel herself shall return to Egypt and to exile in Assyria. (Chs. 9:3, 6; 11:5.) The specific and personal horrors of the coming invasion are foreseen as the will of Yahweh: "Samaria shall bear her guilt, because she has rebelled against her God; they shall fall by the sword, their little ones shall be dashed in pieces, and their pregnant women ripped open" (ch. 13:16). Destruction is promised. "I will destroy you, O Israel; who can help you? Where now is your king, to save you?" (Vs. 9-10.) He shall have perished "like a chip on the face of the waters" (ch. 10:7).

Destruction is not the final word of the prophet. His love for Gomer, his reconciliation with her and the reconstitution of their marriage, Hosea takes as a private oracle from Yahweh concerning his own future dealing with Israel. (Hos. 3:1-4.) "How can I give you up, O Ephraim! How can I hand you over, O Israel! . . . My heart recoils within me, my compassion grows warm and tender. I will not execute my fierce anger, I will not again destroy Ephraim; for I am God and not man, the Holy One in your midst, and I will not come to destroy." (Ch. 11:8-9.) In the final outcome, that is to say, eschatologically, Yahweh will renew his covenant with Israel and will betroth her to himself "in righteousness and in justice, in steadfast love, and in mercy" forever (ch. 2:18-19).

Yet punishment must come. The people must exist for an indefinite time "without king or prince, without sacrifice or pillar, without ephod or teraphim" (Hos. 3:4). Exile cannot be evaded, but eventually the Lord will call his sons from Egypt and from Assyria and return them to their homes. (Ch. 11:10-11.) "In that day" he will abolish the bow, the sword, and war from the land; he will grant harvests abundant and will cause his people to lie down in safety (ch. 2:18-23).[2]

Isaiah. A cultured urbanite intimately associated with the Jerusalem priesthood and with the royal court, Isaiah was, of all the prophets, most discriminatingly loyal to Temple and throne, even when he felt called as the spokesman for Yahweh most bitterly to denounce them. With the exception of Ezekiel, no other prophet so deeply sensed the necessity of institutions for human welfare.

The political horizon of his time was dominated by the expansion of Assyrian imperialism under Tiglath-pileser III (745–727 B.C.), Shalmaneser V (727–722 B.C.), Sargon II (722–705 B.C.), and Sennacherib (705–681 B.C.). In numerous events the Assyrian shadow deeply impinged upon life in Judah and Israel, and consequently upon Isaiah's prophetic message. Assyria was the ultimate target of the abortive Syro-Ephraimitic War, mounted in 734 B.C. against Judah by King Rezin of Syria and Pekah of Israel (Ephraim, from the name of its central district), to overthrow Ahaz and establish in Jerusalem a government favorable to their designs for a coordinated revolt against the Assyrian colossus. A self-confident Hoshea dared later to stop Israel's payment of tribute to the Assyrian crown. In brutal retaliation, Sargon II devastated Hoshea's capital city (721 B.C.), dispersed the elite of his kingdom along the frontiers of the Assyrian realm, and settled upon Samaria the displaced leaders of other peoples restive under the Assyrian yoke. A bit later Hezekiah implicated Judah in a general uprising, signaled by the death of Sargon II. Sennacherib thrust down the revolt. He invaded Judah (ca. 701 B.C.) and smashed the fortifications of forty-six Judean towns — all except those of Jerusalem, which he left standing only upon the condition of the payment of tribute. He then marched swiftly to easy victory over the Egyptian forces upon which Hezekiah had depended.

Isaiah's literary work, found principally but not exclusively in chs. 1 to 11; 14; 17 to 20; 22; 28 to 32 of the book bearing his name, is the product of a long career. His inaugural vision occurred in 742 B.C.: " In the year that King Uzziah died I saw the Lord " (Isa. 6:1). His concluding oracles deal with

Sennacherib's appearance before the walls of Jerusalem in 701 B.C.

A great shift in his message, turning upon the Syro-Ephraimitic war of 734 B.C., marks the close of the first period of his active career. The early oracles of this period are markedly similar in theological and social content to those of Amos, despite differences of style and of audience that sharply distinguish them. Amos spoke to Israel in the blunt speech of the peasant, Isaiah to Jerusalem and Judah in the language of high culture.

Though himself warmly attached to the Temple and its cultus, he could be as scathing as Amos in denouncing a religiosity made to substitute for social justice. (Isa. 1:10-20.) "I have had enough of burnt offerings. . . . Who requires of you this trampling of my courts? . . . I cannot endure iniquity and solemn assembly. Your new moons and your appointed feasts my soul hates. . . . Even though you make many prayers, I will not listen. . . . Cease to do evil, learn to do good; seek justice, correct oppression." Such is the thrust of his oracle from Yahweh. (Vs. 11-17.)

He turns his scorn upon the people of Judah as a whole. He finds them avid patrons of fortune tellers, the willing victims of necromancers. They bargain with foreigners; their affluence is boundless, their armaments massive; they worship the work of their own hands. (Isa. 2:6-8; cf. ch. 8:19.) They are heroes at the bottle. (Ch. 5:22; cf. v. 11.)

No less sharp are his barbed thrusts at the throne. Judah's princes are rebels (a play on words in Hebrew; cf. Hos. 5:10); they all love bribes; they have no concern for the widow and orphan (Isa. 1:23). Her elders and princes are land grabbers; their houses are supplied with the spoil of the poor, whose faces they grind in the dust. (Ch. 3:14-15.) For a bribe, the guilty are acquitted, the innocent is deprived of his rights. (Ch. 5:23.) Oppressive decrees are enacted against the weak and defenseless. (Ch. 10:1-2.) " [The Lord] looked for justice, but behold, bloodshed; for righteousness, but behold, a cry! " (Ch. 5:7.)

Isaiah predicts punishment. In these early oracles, the means of Yahweh's vengeance are equivocal. He will send a vast earthquake (Isa. 2:10, 19; 5:25); the ravages of invasion by enemies unspecified (chs. 3:25 to 4:1; 5:5-7); the terrors of exile to lands unnamed (chs. 5:13, 29; 6:12). In place of affluence and giddy pleasure will come poverty, the stench of decay, signs of mourning, a manhood decimated by the sword. (Chs. 3:24 to 4:1.)

The league between Rezin of Syria and Pekah of Israel against Ahaz panicked Jerusalem. On Isaiah's understanding, the Syro-Ephraimitic crisis cried out for a message of a different sort. The prophet had a child named Shearjashub, meaning "A remnant shall return." Accompanied by this son, whom he had made by name into a living oracle, the prophet intercepted Ahaz on a tour of the city's water supply. He charged his king to be calm, assured him that the foreign conspiracy to place another on his throne would come to nothing, and called for trust in Yahweh, who himself had set limits upon the dominion of his enemies. He closed with a threat implying promise: " If you will not believe, surely you shall not be established " (cf. Isa. 7:1-9; 10:20-21).

At a later meeting he challenged Ahaz to ask for a sign from Yahweh. For his own reasons, the king declined. Isaiah then offered him one: " A young woman [possibly one well known in the royal household] shall conceive and bear a son, and shall call his name Immanuel. . . . Before the child knows how to refuse the evil and choose the good, the land before whose two kings you are in dread will be deserted " (Isa. 7:14-16). Parenthetically, the interpretation of this passage in Matt. 1:18-23 as a messianic oracle referring to a miraculous birth of Jesus is a mistaken reading. In the first place, Isaiah does not intend a miraculous birth. In the second, a birth seven hundred years later, even from a virgin, could hardly serve as a sign for Ahaz in his crisis.

Irked by royal resistance to his counsel, Isaiah subsequently made, for the record, a dramatic public prediction that the Syro-Ephraimitic venture against Judah would end in the defeat of Syria and Israel at the hands of Assyria. (Isa. 8:1-4.) Let the future prove him right or wrong!

Whatever his deficiencies as a Yahwist, as a king in Davidic succession, or as a man, Ahaz must have found exasperating a critic who seemed to counsel dependence upon Yahweh as a specific and fully adequate foreign policy. Unconvinced of the prophet's infallibility, he went about preparation for siege and finally appealed to Assyria for aid against the conspiracy of his neighbors, hastening thereby the fulfillment of Isaiah's prediction of their defeat at Assyrian hands. The price of the aid he sought was enormous tribute, including the silver and gold of the Temple, together with a thorough subordination of Yahwistic to Assyrian cult practices as a token of political subjection. (Cf. II Kings 16:5-19.)

Isaiah's political interpretations derive their coherence from a naïve theological assumption: namely, that Judah's political fortunes are exactly correlative to the purity and impurity of her worship of Yahweh. For this prophet, no victims in history are innocent, even relatively. Political disaster nicely balances breach of faith with God. Foreseeable difficulties in future relations between Judah and Assyria he understood, therefore, as an irony of history. Assyria, the object of Judah's trust in the Syro-Ephraimitic affair, would prove instead to be the instrument of her undoing at the hands of an angry Yahweh. (Cf. Isa. 8:5-8.) Yet, whatever his illusion as to the neat intelligibility of all events in terms of simple divine purpose, Isaiah was realistically skeptical of a people's fear that elevated the enemies of Judah to the status of gods. " Do not fear what they fear, nor be in dread. But the Lord of hosts, him you shall regard as holy; let him be your fear, and let him be your dread." (Cf. vs. 11-13.)

The first period of Isaiah's public ministry ended in 734 B.C. as it began in 742 B.C. upon a note of frustration. (Cf. Isa. 6:9-10.) Petulant at the refusal of his people to make naked confidence in Yahweh their sole reliance against the concerted aggression of Syria and Israel, he sealed his writing for later vindication of his prescience (cf. ch. 9:16 f.) and withdrew into a silence apparently unbroken until, upon the death of Ahaz, Hezekiah ascended the throne.

The oracles preserved from the second period of his public ministry, opening with the ascension of Hezekiah in 715 B.C., constitute primarily a running theological commentary upon the events of the mounting Judeo-Assyrian crisis.

Scarcely had Hezekiah grasped the reins of messianic power when Pharaoh Shabaka ascended the Egyptian throne (ca. 714 B.C.) as founder of the twenty-fifth Ethiopian dynasty. The latter's immediate interest in Eastern Mediterranean politics led Hezekiah among others to expect a shift in the balance of power. Deluded by this prospect, the coastal kingdom of Ashdod in 713 B.C. revolted against Assyria, expecting Egyptian aid which never came — against inevitable reprisal. Judah and her fellow conspirators withdrew from the Ashdod plot only just in time.[3] In the year that Sargon II finally dealt with the revolt (711 B.C.), Isaiah paraded naked through the streets of Jerusalem to dramatize his prediction that Assyria would lead Egypt and Ethiopia into exile. (Isa. 20:1-6.)

The uprising following Sargon's death in 705 B.C. found Hezekiah an active party to a Palestinian alliance with Egypt against Assyria. Apparently, Isaiah had already exposed the existence of the secret pact (Isa. 29:15), which he called a covenant with death (ch. 28:18). The alliance, he declared, would fail (vs. 18-22); Egypt's help was worthless (ch. 30:7). His critique of the alliance reads in part like a protest against diplomacy and arms used for sheer political power as an end in itself. " Egyptians are men, and not God; and their horses are flesh, and not spirit." (Ch. 31:3; cf. ch. 30:12.) As such a protest, it comprises a timely corrective of political ideologies in every age. Yet it reads also like a demand for naked dependence upon Yahweh as one precisely political possibility among all other political possibilities, which it supplants. (Cf. chs. 30:15-16; 31:1-5.) This demand comprises a theological illusion as potentially destructive as the ideology of messianic kingship, of which it is the correlate.

Assyrian imperialism appears to the prophet as the rod of Yahweh's wrath against Judah, the tragedies great and small of invasion as willed by God. (Isa. 10:5.) Yet Assyria serves as an unwitting agent, whose arrogance in turn will be punished. (Vs. 7, 12-16.) In a little while the Lord's indignation toward Judah will be ended, his anger directed toward Assyrian destruction. (Vs. 24-27.) A funeral pyre is prepared for her king. (Ch. 30:33.) Yahweh purposes to break the Assyrian in his land, to liberate Judah, indeed to free all peoples from the burden of the Assyrian yoke, for his hand is stretched out over all the nations. (Ch. 14:24-27.)

In the course of suppressing the general uprising sparked by his predecessor's death, Sennacherib appeared in 701 B.C. before the walls of Jerusalem. Upon Hezekiah's payment of tribute, he spared the city. (II Kings 18:14-16.) Legend has it, however, that he lifted his siege because a pestilence destroyed his army (Isa. 37:36) — a notorious instance of the reconstruction of history in the interest of piety. Later events only partially honored Isaiah's prediction that Sennacherib would "fall by a sword, not of man" (Isa. 31:8). Twenty years after the siege, the king died by the sword in fact, wielded, however, in the hands of his sons.

Several oracles of uncertain date, traditionally ascribed to Isaiah, have left their mark upon the changing messianic interpretation of history. Two of them, Isa. 9:2-7 and 11:1-9, long interpreted as intending Jesus of Nazareth, may well be genuinely Isaianic. If genuine, they apparently served as oracular accreditation of specific Judean kings at their enthronement.[4] Their use in Christian liturgy as predictions fulfilled by the Christmas story thus violates their original intent.

Numerous other oracles, debatably ascribed to Isaiah, project a definitely messianic eschatology; that is to say, they clearly predict an end (eschaton) of the present situation and the beginning of a messianic age through Yahweh's miraculous transformation of nature and of history. A few of these may well come from Isaiah himself in his old age.[5] If Isa. 2:2-5 originates with him, he predicts " in the latter days " a Yahwistic religious imperialism as the foundation of a warless world. If ch. 11:10 is his, he promises that " in that day " the messianic ideology of a Davidic world imperialism will be realized. Of the eschatological oracles traditionally ascribed to Isaiah, none rejects Davidic political messianism or the Temple cultus as the human agents of the divine reign in the coming age. The messianism of the eschatological future is still messianic royalism — purged, however, of its past defections from Yahweh.

Isaiah's theology emerges as basically the ideology of messianic kingship ethically refined and mated with an otherwise realistic appraisal of the political situation in his day. Monarchy provides his most forceful symbols of the transcendent glory of Yahweh. " I saw the Lord sitting upon a throne, high and lifted up. . . . And I said: ' Woe is me! . . . For my eyes have seen the King, the Lord of hosts! ' " (Isa. 6:1, 5.) Yahweh alone shall be exalted. Before him the self-exaltation of the haughty will be humbled, their pretentious transcendence denied. (Chs. 2:17; 5:15.) His exaltation, the dreadful fascination of his holiness, stems from inexorable justice, and not from naked power. (Ch. 5:16.) Though hidden from the unseeing (chs. 5:12; 29:14), that justice holds sovereign sway in all the affairs of men.

On these assumptions, the fact of catastrophe excludes the possibility of innocence; the terrors of imperialism can have no explanation except guilt before God. Yahweh it is who sifts the nations with the sieve of destruction. (Isa. 30:28.) Even arrogant Assyria, unwitting, performs his " alien work " (ch. 28:21). " I send him. . . . But he does not so intend." (Ch. 10:6-7.) Because her imperium is promoted for its own sake, and not for the sake of universal justice (vs. 5-16), Assyria will be broken and the nations freed of her rule (ch. 14:24-27).

This is not to suggest that Isaiah envisioned a radically liberal world order. There is no evidence that he saw anything inherently injurious to the dignity of men in the political and religious imperialism implicit within the Davidic covenant. His vision of the equality of nations before Yahweh somehow always implies that Judah is " more equal than others."

Jeremiah. The prophetic activity of Jeremiah, more than that of any prophet before or after him, meshed directly into the current events of his day. His oracles cluster around four military episodes, all of them related to the disintegration of Assyrian power and the rise of Babylonian power, all of them bearing upon the destiny of messianic royalism in Judah. They comprise the Battle of Megiddo, 609 B.C.; the Battle of Carchemish, 605 B.C.; the siege of Jerusalem by Babylon and the first deportation of Judean exiles, 598–597 B.C.; the second siege, ending in the destruction of the Temple and city, 587 B.C.

After Josiah fell at Megiddo in 609 B.C., his son Jehoiakim was enthroned by victorious Neco as vassal king of Judah. Jeremiah's first major address, delivered in the same year within the Temple, was an attack upon the Temple itself, both as a symbol of political security and as an assured place of Yahweh's benign dwelling. " Your morals turn to mockery your worship of Yahweh in this house," was the substance of his charge. " Deluded is your trust in the magic of the words: ' This is the temple of the Lord, the temple of the Lord, the temple of the Lord.' Unless you amend your ways," was his oracle from Yahweh, " I will do to this house and this place as I did to Shiloh, where first I made my dwelling. I will cast you out as I cast out your kinsmen, all the offspring of Ephraim." (Jer.7:1-15; 26:2-6.)

Horror and fury greeted his Temple address. We learn from Baruch's memoirs that prophets, priests, and people seized Jeremiah and hastened him to trial before the princes, quickly assembled. There he narrowly escaped the death sentence. Fortunately for Jeremiah, one of the elders remembered that under Hezekiah, Micah's prediction of the destruction of Jerusalem (Micah 3:12) had gone unpunished (cf. Jer. 26:7-24).

The Temple sermon, in shocking effect, declared the actual achievements of Josiah's regime no longer relevant, its central aims aborted. The centralizing of Yahwistic worship in the Temple and the defiant banning from it of all foreign gods served in 622 B.C. to measure Assyrian decadence rather more than Judean political stature. Josiah's last defiance of Assyria at Megiddo had cost his life and the defeat of his army by Neco of Egypt, under whose hegemony Judah now came. True, his engagement of Egyptian forces at the famous pass left Assyria to deal unaided with a rebellious Babylon. Yet even this partial success of his military stratagem made pointless his earlier symbolic defiance in matters of worship. Purging the Temple of Assyrian gods would count for nothing against the rising ambitions of Babylon.

The announced heart of the Josiah reformation had fared even worse than its muted political aims. The basic socioethical and legal reforms, called for by the Deuteronomic theological revival undergirding the movement, apparently failed of implementation. (Jer. 7:5-12.) Although suppression of the old Canaanitic local deities had been a major purpose of centralized Yahwism, their worship still flourished; even human sacrifice had been revived (vs. 16-34). Public clamor resounding to Jeremiah's attack upon Temple ideology only echoed his striking of an empty symbol, a hollow reform.

At Carchemish upon the Euphrates in 605 B.C., Babylon finally met and routed the combined forces of Egypt and Assyria (cf. Jer. 46:2). Egypt's defeat is celebrated by the prophet in a vindictive oracle found in vs. 3-12. The petty kingdoms of Palestine, among them Judah, by prompt payment of tribute acknowledged Babylonian control.

Debarred from the Temple at the time, Jeremiah dictated to his scribe Baruch for recording on a scroll his commentary upon the new developments of 605. In these oracles he castigated Judah in a bill of particulars and specified her coming destruction by Nebuchadnezzar of Babylon. Waiting almost a year for a suitable occasion, he sent Baruch to the Temple to read the scroll before a large public gathering. News of the oracles and of their origin spread quickly and soon the scroll was brought before Jehoiakim's royal council. As the reading of the scroll progressed three or four columns at a time, the king with a penknife cut off the portion last read and burned it in the fire of a brazier until the whole was consumed. Jeremiah later dictated his work all over again (the core of our present book), adding oracles in similar vein, among them a prediction of Jehoiakim's ignominious death. (Cf. Jer., ch. 36.)

In this period, apparently, the prophet clashed with Pashhur, a prophetic priest of the Temple retinue who envisioned for Judah a more hopeful future, dependent presumably upon Egyptian aid. To teach the arrogant Jeremiah a lesson, he once had him locked overnight in the Temple stocks. Upon his release, characteristically, Jeremiah reiterated his threat of Judah's destruction, predicting that Pashhur would be among the exiles to die and be buried in Babylon. (Jer. 20:1-6.)

Just three years had passed since Carchemish and Nebuchadnezzar's accession when Jehoiakim, upon the advice of his favored prophets and counselors, withheld tribute to Babylon. (II Kings 24:1.) His death (598 B.C.) during the resultant siege of Jerusalem is the subject of a vitriolic oracle by Jeremiah. (Jer. 22:13-19.) His son and successor, Jehoiachin (Jeconiah, Coniah), reigned for three months until the walls of the city were breached, its treasures looted, in 597 B.C. Then among 3,023 Jewish elite (Jer. 29:2; 52:28) young Jehoiachin was deported into Babylon. Threatened exile had become a fact. Jeremiah honored him and the queen mother in brief lament (Jer. 13:15-19) and predicted his death in captivity with no descendant to succeed him on the throne of David (Jer. 22:24-30). In the meanwhile, Nebuchadnezzar placed Jehoiachin's uncle, Mattaniah, a puppet whom he renamed Zedekiah (II Kings 24:17), over Judah.

Around 594 B.C. negotiations were afoot for a pan-Palestinian revolt against Babylon, involving Zedekiah. Jeremiah carved and wore around his neck a yoke to enforce a message sent to the conspirators through their emissaries in Jerusalem. Nebuchadnezzar, he declared, was the servant of Yahweh, to whom the Lord had given the nations of the earth. Those who refused to bow the neck under his yoke Yahweh himself would destroy by famine, pestilence, and sword. Those nations who wore his yoke Yahweh would leave on their own land, to till it and dwell there. (Jer. 27:1-11.) He singled out Zedekiah for a similar warning. (Vs. 12-22.) Against the prevailing counsel of his fellow prophets, he urged as the will of Yahweh, " Serve the king of Babylon and live " (v. 17).

Later in the same year, this clash among the prophets flared up dramatically in public. Confronting Jeremiah in the presence of priests and people in the Temple, Hananiah predicted the return, within two years, of the Temple vessels, of King Jeconiah and all the exiles, for Yahweh " will break the yoke of the king of Babylon." After mulling that one over, Jeremiah, as his oracle from Yahweh, sent word to Hananiah: " You have broken wooden bars, but I will make in their place bars of iron." As a grim afterthought, he predicted Hananiah's death within the year. Baruch reports that Hananiah obliged by dying. (Jer., ch. 28.)

Sometime early in Zedekiah's reign, Jeremiah sent by courtesy of a royal messenger a letter to the exiles themselves. He urged that they build houses, plant gardens, marry, have children and promote their marriages, seek the advantage of the city of their exile, " for in its welfare you will find your welfare." Opposing the prophets among them, he predicted a long stay in Babylon. (Jer. 29:1-9.)

His warnings were not long effective against the party promoting rebellious alliance with Egypt. In retaliation for the second withholding of tribute, Nebuchadnezzar mounted the disastrous siege of 588 B.C. (opening possibly in December of 589 B.C.). Jeremiah confidently forecast the fall of Jerusalem, its burning, and Zedekiah's exile. The prospect of natural death and honorable burial was the one small comfort he extended to Judah's king. (Jer. 34:1-7.)

As a defense measure early in the siege, Zedekiah proclaimed freedom for all Hebrews in slavery to their fellow countrymen, only to revoke the order when the Babylonians lifted their attack to meet an approaching Egyptian army. The prophet's bitter denunciation of this perfidy is preserved in vs. 8-22.

While the siege was suspended, Zedekiah, through an emissary, requested Jeremiah's prayers for Jerusalem. The prophet responded by announcing Yahweh's plans for the withdrawal of Pharaoh's army into Egypt, Babylon's resumption of the siege and burning of the city. (Jer. 37:1-10.)

Before Nebuchadnezzar's forces had returned to the attack, Jeremiah sought to leave the capital, apparently to conduct some personal business in the town of his birth, Anathoth. He was arrested at the city gate for attempted desertion to the enemy and thrown into a prison dungeon. (Vs. 11-15.) Shortly, he was summoned to a secret interview with Zedekiah, who inquired: " Is there any word from the Lord? " " There is," he replied. " You shall be delivered into the hand of the king of Babylon." He prevailed upon the king to move him from the dungeon to more spacious and public quarters in the court of the guard (vs. 16-21), where he remained until the city fell (Jer. 38:28). Here he urged all who would listen to desert to the enemy. To stop this attack upon the morale of the defending soldiers, the princes obtained royal authority to kill the prophet. He was saved from death in the mire of an empty cistern only through the connivance of the king himself. (Vs. 1-13.)

He was shortly summoned to a second hush-hush interview, in which he conveyed Yahweh's promise to spare Jerusalem, the king and his family, upon the condition of their surrender to Babylon — otherwise, torch and exile. Zedekiah refused the challenge, pleading fear of the Jews who already had deserted to the enemy. (Vs. 14-28.)

While still imprisoned, Jeremiah announced his hope for the future of Judah by buying a field from his cousin and sealing the deed in a jar for long safekeeping. " For thus says the Lord of hosts, the God of Israel: Houses and fields and vineyards shall again be bought in this land." (Jer. 32:1-15.)

In 587 B.C. the defenses of Jerusalem were breached, the

Temple destroyed, the city burned, its walls razed. Zedekiah, captured in flight, was taken before Nebuchadnezzar at Riblah, where he witnessed the slaughter of the leaders of Judah's revolt, including his sons, only to be himself then blinded. Among 832 of his fellow Jews, he was taken to exile in Babylon, where he died in prison. (Jer., ch. 52.)

Upon capturing Jerusalem, the besiegers delivered Jeremiah from prison into the custody of Gedaliah (Jer. 39:14), whom they installed as governor of Judah. Jewish resistance forces soon assassinated Gedaliah, together with a spate of fellow collaborationists and a group of occupation forces who chanced to be on the scene at the time. Fearful of indiscriminate reprisals, a collection of Judeans fled to Egypt, dragging Jeremiah along as a sort of hostage. We last hear of him as he fulminates against his fellow Jews in Egypt (chs. 42 to 44), predicting that Nebuchadnezzar as the servant of Yahweh will conquer the Nile and erect his royal canopy over the very stones that Jeremiah ostentatiously had buried in the pavement of the court before Pharaoh's palace (ch. 43:8-10). Quite understandable, whether true or not, is the legend that his irate compatriots finally stoned him to death.

A fiery theological fanaticism pervades the speech and action of Jeremiah toward the people and throne of Judah. His mixture of shrewd realism and distorted logic both probes the actual functions of Judean messianic royalism in its final stages, and at the same time exposes in grotesque exaggeration the strength and weakness of the prophetic movement in Hebrew life.

His conception of his prophetic role clearly exhibits delusions of grandeur analogous to those implicit within the ideology of messianic royalism itself. On his understanding, the oracle of Yahweh spoken by the prophet causes the events of history to happen. Not the king, but the true prophet manipulates the peoples of the earth: " Behold, I have put my words in your mouth. See, I have set you this day over nations and over kingdoms, to pluck up and to break down, to destroy and to overthrow, to build and to plant " (Jer. 1:9-10).

In the counterphase of this theological megalomania, he hates himself, curses the day he was born, damns the man who brought news of his birth for not having slain him unborn so that his mother's womb could have been his tomb. " Why did I come forth from the womb to see toil and sorrow, and spend my days in shame? " (Jer. 20:14-18.)

A parallel ambivalence marks his relations with others. More eloquently than any other prophet, he laments the suffering of his people. Yet his very expressions of sorrow, couched in the language of his private suffering, only thinly veil his hatred toward those whom he mourns. (Cf. Jer. 9:1-6; 13:15-19.) When his pronouncements of doom are challenged, he lashes out in undisguised fury against the very hearers for whom his oracles of warning are intended: " I am making my words in your mouth a fire, and this people wood, and the fire shall devour them," is his private word from Yahweh. (Ch. 5:12-14.) Vengeful prayers for the destruction of his personal enemies (chs. 17:18; 20:12; 28:16) are not enough; his unrelenting hatred requires catastrophe for their wives and children as well (chs. 18:21-23; 20:6).

The polarization of his personal existence between oppressive self-negation and violent self-affirmation, whatever its psychogenesis, has its theological source in his conception of Yahweh and of Yahweh's relation to history. History, he implies, is thoroughly rational, the actually existing situation ultimately right. For Yahweh made heaven and earth, its men and animals; their actual distribution from age to age is by his sovereign action, according to his own standards of justice. (Jer. 27:5.) Nebuchadnezzar's wide dominion constitutes presumptive evidence that he acts as Yahweh's agent in history. It is God who has placed upon the neck of nations the iron yoke of servitude to Babylon. Bow to the inevitable as to the will of God. (Chs. 27:6-11; 28:13-14.) Parenthetically, on the premise that ultimately Yahweh does all that is done in world history, twenty million dead Jews in a later era would seem to prove that Hitler was somehow on God's side.

He uses Isaiah's figure of the potter and his clay (Isa. 29:16) to picture Yahweh as an absolute sovereign creatively engaged with subjects genuinely free before him (Jer. 18:1-11). The crude comparison of people to clay accents the basic contradiction in his theology.

When his emphasis falls upon the absoluteness of the divine sovereignty, he portrays human impotence before the evil forces of history as man's helplessness before God. Evil is God's doing. (Jer. 15:10-13.) (Yahweh himself is infected by the very sickness for which man needs the cure.) War against Judah, he identifies without remainder as a punitive act of God. (Chs. 6:1-6; 8:16.) Yahweh, he supposes, wills even the multitudinous personal bereavements and terrors of the civilian population incident to war. (Chs. 15:5-9; 14:16; 6:11-12.)

When he stresses human freedom and the conditional character of the divine decision, he quickly falls victim of the prophetic fallacy. The supposed lucid intelligibility of history, as he views it, functions singularly around Yahweh's involvement in the parochial affairs of tiny Judah. If only she turns back to him, Yahweh will reverse for her sake the obvious course of world history. (Jer. 26:3, 13.)

Jeremiah's career itself enacts the logic of the premise that calamity constitutes without remainder Yahweh's punishment of human conduct. When disaster threatens, he calls for amended behavior; when it strikes, he counsels willing endurance of the merited wrath of God. His theology finds its central problem in suffering and guilt, its key in his conception of justice.

Alike for Jeremiah and his prophetic predecessors, the Hebrew term for justice and its equivalents signify loyalty between Yahweh and the whole of Israel — loyalty based on the covenant established and maintained between them out of Yahweh's love and mercy toward his chosen people. To them he is God in the way that a loyal man is father to his son or husband to his wife. The life of Yahweh and Israel together is properly a know-ing each of the other. All dimensions of human life are ele-vated into this divine-human relationship. The specific content of justice between persons, therefore, in both face-to-face and institutional encounter, derives from and depends upon the dy-namic character and purpose of Yahweh. Injustice correspond-ingly signifies any breach of covenant by human behavior dis-loyal to what Yahweh purposes and is actually doing in the af-fairs of men. Despite its grotesque illusions, this Hebraic theological tradition is distinguished from the like traditions of surrounding cultures, from which it is borrowed, by a compara-tive openness to what goes on in the depth of history, by a ca-pacity for self-correction in the light of experience, by greater sensitivity to certain human values.

In Jeremiah, for the first time in Biblical literature, the justice of Yahweh is challenged. He likens Yahweh, " the fountain of living water," to a deceitful brook whose waters fail (Jer. 15:18). " Righteous art thou, O Lord, when I complain to thee; yet I would plead my case before thee. Why does the way of the wicked prosper? Why do all who are treacherous thrive? Thou plantest them, and they take root; they grow and bring forth fruit; thou art near in their mouth and far from their heart." (Ch. 12:1-2.) His fanatic longing for the swift slaughter of the wicked perhaps measures a skepticism deeper than he dares openly to utter. In any case, he pleads his own suffering as that of a comparatively righteous man. (Ch. 12:3-4; cf. ch. 15:15-19.)

The thrust of his theology, however, remains conservative. Like his predecessors of the eighth century, he is obsessed by the sufferings of Judah and Israel under the impact of cataclys-mic imperial power. Though he questions implicitly the tradi-tional view of that suffering, he is open to no other answer. Ca-tastrophe is still for him the measured justice of God. To a cata-logue of national disaster he appends this word from Yahweh to Judah: " Because your guilt is great, . . . I have done these things to you " (Jer. 30:15).

His running critique of messianic kingship in Judah, he conducts within the framework of his general theory of suffering, i.e., within his theodicy. He takes the art of politics literally as religion, for the throne comprises for him an integral part of the whole complex Yahwistic religious establishment. In calling his king to execute justice by delivering from the hand of the oppressor him who has been robbed, he invokes theological rather than narrowly moral or political sanctions (Jer. 21:12). His blistering condemnation of Jehoiakim for " eyes and heart only for your dishonest gain, for shedding innocent blood, and for practicing oppression and violence " burns with indignation at conduct indeed immoral, but for him the more heinous because unholy (ch. 22:13-19) and beyond the bounds of knowledgeable intercourse with God. He blames Judah's predicament upon the ineptitude of her rulers. Yet he finds in their stupidity more than a lack of military and diplomatic intelligence; they make no inquiry after Yahweh. (Ch. 10:21.) On the premise that history exhibits exactly what Yahweh is doing, failure to know him is the crowning stupidity.

He castigates not only kings and princes, but priests, prophets (Jer. 2:8, 26), and people alike (ch. 5:30-31). He excoriates idolatry, which he portrays, unoriginally, under the analogies of harlotry. (Chs. 2:28; 3:1, 13; 5:7.) He is bitter against the cult of the Canaanitic queen of heaven (ch. 7:17-18), appalled at the practice of human sacrifice (vs. 31-34; cf. ch. 44:16 ff.). He rejects frankincense, sacrifices, burnt offerings; they are inappropriate to the worship of Yahweh. (Chs. 6:30; 7:21-22.) He can contemplate the destruction of the Temple as no loss to essential Yahwism. Circumcision, to be valid, must be a circumcision of the heart. (Chs. 4:4; 9:26.) He calls, in short, for a life that shall itself be a liturgy of loyal obedience to the word of Yahweh. (Chs. 7:23; 6:19.)

His heaviest verbal barrages, when not aimed at the throne, are fired at the prophetic quacks who had largely taken over his own profession. " An appalling and horrible thing has happened in the land: the prophets prophesy falsely, and the priests rule at their direction; my people love to have it so." (Jer. 5:30-31.)

The prophetic charlatans of Samaria, he recalls, were an unsavory lot; but those of Jerusalem are more thoroughly pernicious. (Ch. 23:13-14.) Theistic harlots, all of them (v. 14), they ply their trade without real knowledge of Yahweh (ch. 14:18).

In world affairs, they have no word from the Lord, but speak instead the empty hopes, the lying dreams and deceitful visions of their own minds. (Jer. 23:16, 26, 32.) They prescribe for superficial healing and ignore the deep wound of the nation, " saying ' Peace, peace,' when there is no peace." (Chs. 6:14; 8:10-11.)

Like the great prophets whom he consciously emulated, Jeremiah viewed with a measure of unflinching political realism the world crisis of his age. As for the prophet who predicts peace, when the word of that prophet comes to pass, then it will be known that Yahweh has truly sent him. (Jer. 28:8-9.) This is not to suggest that prophecy is properly interpreted in purely political, psychological, or other such terms. Jeremiah is an ideologist, or if one prefers, a theologist, whose theological vision is warped by illusory premises, namely, that Yahweh unequivocally wills what is for us now inevitable, and that resistance to the inevitable is, therefore, obdurately wrong. When he counsels Judah to knuckle under to Nebuchadnezzar, he speaks neither as a pacifist nor as the first quisling, but rather as a theologian who may have been theologically right for some quite wrong theological reasons.

In domestic affairs, according to Jeremiah, the prophetic sycophants of Jerusalem gave an air of legitimacy to the corrupted morals of the people, strengthening the hand of the evildoer. (Jer. 23:14, 17.) Even her century-long possession of the written Torah, he saw, gave Judah no assured wisdom as to the mind of Yahweh, for the false pen of the scribes had made the very law of the Lord into a lie. (Ch. 8:8.)

" My people love to have it so." Jeremiah searches the streets of Jerusalem for a man who does justice and seeks truth. He finds only unrepentant faces, harder than rock. (Jer. 5:1-3.) He consoles himself. The masses have no sense; he will look for the

knowledge of Yahweh among the great of the city. But all alike
have broken the yoke and burst their ties with the Lord (vs.
4-5); he finds nothing but oppression in her (ch. 6:6). Every
one of the people as a whole, from least to greatest, is greedy
for unfair profit. (Chs. 6:13; 8:10.) They are slanderers, sup-
planters, deceivers, liars; " heaping oppression upon oppression,
and deceit upon deceit, they refuse to know me, says the Lord."
(Ch. 9:4-6.)

Scholarly debate as to authorship of material in our present
book somewhat beclouds reconstruction of Jeremiah's view on
the final outcome of Yahweh's affair with Judah and Israel —
the end of it all. As in the case of earlier prophets, anonymous
commentators of the postexilic era occasionally have inserted
their own eschatological comments into the work of Jeremiah,
until public esteem of his writings eventually closed them to such
interpolations. A majority of scholars concur in attributing a
few eschatological oracles to Jeremiah's own pen.

Among the latter is one declaring Yahweh's mercy toward
Ephraim, " my dear son, my darling child," and promising that
Hebrew exiles from Northern Israel will sometime return from
the land of the enemy. (Jer. 31:16-22.) He probably composed
also the beautiful lines of vs. 2-6, an oracle of Yahweh's love
and promised restoration of a virgin and undivided Israel.

Jeremiah generally is credited with the substance, if not with
the present language, of the oracle concerning the new eschatological covenant between Yahweh and a reunited Israel, the sign
of which will be the writing of the law of the Lord upon human
hearts rather than (as at first) upon stone. (Vs. 31-34.) [6] This
individualizing of a divine-human relationship that still remains
also basically social constitutes a bench mark in prophetic
thought. In vs. 29-30, dubiously attributable to the prophet, occurs a stronger emphasis upon individual responsibility before
God in the eschatological situation — so strong, in fact, that the
social dimension of personal existence is in effect denied.

The place of the Davidic messianic dynasty in the *eschaton,*
though little discussed, is apparently taken for granted. The mes-

sianic oracle in Jer. 23:5-6, the authenticity of which is much
debated by scholars,[7] conveys Yahweh's promise to raise up for
David in days to come a righteous branch who shall deal wisely
and execute justice. The Hebrew word for "branch" may be
here construed as a play on the name Zedekiah. By inference,
the eschatological king is distinguished from his predecessors
simply by the fact that where they only pretend righteousness,
he will be actually righteous. Nothing in the oracle conflicts either with the ideology of messianic royalism or with the theology of Jeremiah.

Jeremiah's writing gives no evidence of substantial erosion or
transformation of the ideology of messianic kingship. Quite original and potentially disruptive is his question as to the justice of
Yahweh's dealing in human affairs. Despite that question, however, and despite his new accent upon the individual's relation
with Yahweh, his theology of history remains basically a prophetic refinement and correlate of messianic royalism itself.
This holds true even in his sober, down-to-earth eschatology.

Ezekiel. Despite an impressive consensus on many details, exceptional controversy still plagues all efforts fully to recover
from the present book of Ezekiel the work originating with Ezekiel himself. No less controversial are attempts to determine the
original order of the material and to reconstruct the career of
the prophet.

We know that he was a priest (Ezek. 1:3), probably of the
prestigious Zadokite order stemming from the Zadok of David's
court who took part with Nathan in the anointing of Solomon (I
Kings 1:39, 45). He seems to have been among the exiles of
597 B.C., deported by Nebuchadnezzar into Babylon. We have
two accounts of his prophetic commission (Ezek. 1:2-3 and
3:4-9), each referring, presumably, to his ecstatic vision in the
fifth year of the exile (592 B.C.) by the river Chebar in Babylon.
We find no conclusive evidence of his prophetic activity prior to
that date. Neither do we find conclusive evidence that he was
ever again actually in Jerusalem after his exile. Several of his

dramatized oracles of doom, however, strongly imply either that he was prophesying in Jerusalem prior to Nebuchadnezzar's siege of 597, or else prior to the punitive destruction of the city in 587. In the former case, he started his prophetic career before the exile; in the latter and more probable case, he revisited his homeland sometime during his banishment. His knowledge of the exact date on which the final siege of Jerusalem was mounted suggests that he was present on the scene (Ezek. 24:1-2). In any case, he seems intimately familiar with conditions in Jerusalem during the Babylonian captivity, whether in part by first-hand knowledge or wholly by report we cannot now be certain. The latest among a dozen or so dates supplied for his occasional oracles is the twenty-seventh year of the exile or 570 B.C. (Ezek. 29:17),[8] indicating a career of some twenty-two years.

Of the four sections of the present book, the first (chs. 1 to 24) opens with a vision of the destructive power of Yahweh's glory. Ezekiel reports seeing in his inaugural ecstasy a storm out of which loomed cherubim and wheels whirling within wheels, supporting a dome not unlike the vault of the sky, surmounted in turn by Yahweh's throne upon which sat the brilliance of the divine presence, portrayed to the reader in guardedly anthropomorphic language. (Ch. 1:4-28; cf. ch. 10:1-22.) The prophet is ordered into the midst of the wheels to take burning coals from between the cherubim and scatter them over Jerusalem.

Next we read about several dramatic predictions of the coming doom of Judah. Upon the clay of an unbaked brick the prophet portrays the siege of Jerusalem. (Ezek. 4:1-3.) He eats and drinks the measured rations of the besieged. (Vs. 9-17.) The hair of his head and face he shaves off with a sharp sword, disposing of the hair in ways symbolic of war. (Ch. 5:1-4.) He likens the city to a caldron containing, like meat to be cooked, the bodies of the slain (ch. 11:7; cf. ch. 23:3-5); a pot to be emptied of unwholesome broth and itself purified by fire (ch. 24:10-11). He digs through the wall and leaves the city, bearing an exile's baggage to signify the coming fate of the citizens of Judah and especially of their king. (Ch. 12:1-14.) He erects signposts directing Nebuchadnezzar's troops to Jerusalem. (Ch. 21:18-23.)

In a medley of allegories, he mirrors the political situation and expands the theme of doom, familiar since the days of Amos. He likens Judah to the worthless wood of a vine (Ezek. 15:1-6). He treats of Hebrew historical origins in terms of bastardy and expands the now trite metaphor of harlotry (ch. 16:1-47), comparing Samaria and Judah to fallen virgins, sisters Oholah and Oholibah (ch. 23). The figure of the Lion of Judah he converts to acid satire (ch. 19:1-9); he even turns the death of his wife into a ghastly advertisement of the coming profanation of the Temple (ch. 24:15-23).

Most of the oracles against the nations comprising the second section (Ezek., chs. 25 to 32) are either spurious or else greatly modified by hands other than Ezekiel's. Probably genuine are the poetic portions of the dirge for fallen Tyre, in which she is compared to a superbly constructed, manned, and cargoed ship sunk at sea (ch. 27:3-9, 25-36). Securely ascribed to Ezekiel is the oracle against the king of Tyre (ch. 28:11-19).[9] We seem to have authentic Ezekiel also in the poetry of the oracles against Egypt and her king (chs. 30:1 to 32:19). Egypt's wealth will be Nebuchadnezzar's plunder. (Ch. 30:10 f.) "You consider yourself a lion among the nations, but you are like a dragon in the seas." Because you have befouled the rivers of the earth, you are doomed. (Ch. 32:2 f.)

At some point in his career, now uncertain, Ezekiel turned from utterances of guilt and destruction to promises of an Israel restored and sustained by the gracious goodwill of Yahweh. Section three of the present book (Ezek., chs. 33 to 39) portrays the envisioned renaissance as centered in the Davidic dynasty, restored and fulfilling in modest reality many of the characteristic claims of Hebrew messianic ideology. With the possible exception of the vision of the valley of dry bones (ch. 37:1-14), the extent of Ezekiel's contribution to this section remains in debate.[10]

The last section (Ezek., chs. 40 to 48) culminates in a vision of the river of life, gushing from the Temple in Jerusalem, making paradise of Palestine, and freshening even the waters of the Dead Sea (ch. 47:1-12). Assurance is given to the salt-mining interests, however, that the fresh water will not affect the surrounding marshes and salt flats. Detailed plans are projected for rebuilding the Temple and proposals advanced for a community life largely dominated by Zadokite priests. (Chs. 43:18-27; 44:15-31, *et passim*.) The Levites, however, who formerly served at shrines in the outlying provinces of Judah, are to be demoted from full priestly status and consigned to lesser service in the Temple, presumably because of corrupt and heathen practices indulged in at Jerusalem while the Zadokites were in exile. (Ch. 44:10-14.) The section as it stands foresees the restoration of the monarchy with legal restraints upon former abuses of power. (Cf. chs. 43:6-9; 45:7-8; 46:16-18.)

Following traditions of prophetic protest, Ezekiel lashes out against all phases of the Jewish establishment. He scores whitewashing prophets for seeing false visions, divining lies, crying, " Peace," when there is no peace, and making many a widow in Israel, presumably by their sanction of ill-advised foreign adventures of the throne. (Ezek. 13:8-16; 22:25, 28.) He damns priests and elders for the resurgence of scandalous religiosity, debased to the point of human sacrifice. (Ch. 16:15-21; cf. chs. 8:5-18; 22:26.)

His bitterest scorn he reserves for the monarchy. More vigorously than Hosea or Isaiah, he condemns foreign alliances as one aspect of harlotrous disloyalty to Yahweh. (Ezek. 23:1-34.) Harshly he denounces Zedekiah's pact with Egypt as the breach of a prior covenant with Nebuchadnezzar and with Yahweh. In this affair, the prophet stands convinced that Yahweh wills Judah's vassalage to Babylon as her punishment, and he remembers that Nebuchadnezzar had made Zedekiah subscribe to his terms with an oath in Yahweh's name. (Ezek. 17:18-19; cf. II Chron. 36:13.) Unlike his predecessors, he pokes fun at the pretensions of royalty. Referring to Judah as a lioness (" What a lioness . . . among lions! ") and to her kings as lion whelps, he satirizes the hollowness of messianic ideology by extolling the quite puny achievements of Jehoahaz and Jehoiachin: " The land was appalled and all who were in it at the sound of his roaring." (Ezek. 19:1-9.) Each reigned for three calamitous months, the former to be deposed by Neco and exiled in Egypt, the latter to be deposed by Nebuchadnezzar and exiled in Babylon. The human pride of empire he bitterly mocks in a funeral dirge for Egypt and her multitudes slain by sword and descended into the Pit of the lower world — joining there the Assyrians, Elamites, Edomites, and Sidonians who in their times have terrorized the nations. (Ch. 32:17-32.) The princes of Judah are no exception; they, too, are a grasping and bloodthirsty lot. (Ch. 22:27.)

Though he directs his shafts without hesitation at every monarch on his horizon, yet he leaves no clear evidence that he repudiated the monarchic institution itself. His elegy for the king of Tyre opens with adulation for the latent promise, even the divine potentialities, of the king's career. He does not lament the fact of royal sovereignty, but rather he bemoans in this king's actual achievements the abuses of power (Ezek. 28:11-19).

Significant consequences for social and theological history turn upon the perhaps insoluble question whether Ezekiel finally came out for a theocracy exercised through priestcraft exclusively or for one in which kingcraft had a part as well. Some Old Testament scholars argue, largely upon the basis of debated linguistic and stylistic evidence, that references to the restoration of the Davidic dynasty are without exception the work of Ezekiel's late editor. They conclude that the prophet envisioned the reconstituted Hebrew theocracy as exclusively priestly in character. More numerous are those who attribute to Ezekiel himself, for example, the oracle of the two sticks joined to symbolize Judah and Israel reunited under the house of David restored.[11] If the oracle is properly ascribed to Ezekiel's pen, he centers renascent Hebrew theocracy both in Temple and throne (Ezek. 37:24-28), with the latter limited to block the more obvious abuses of the scepter. The dual arrangement seems more probable, if for no other reason than the lack of a definitive trace of so radical a repudiation of the monarchic system. In no case, however, does the prophet ever surmount the simplistic notion that the course of human events is largely determined by the dynamics of Yahweh's affair with the Hebrews and that for them the events of history are a direct function of their guilt or innocence before God.

PROPHECIES OF YAHWEH'S RECONSTITUTION OF ISRAEL

Second Isaiah. This prophet was by no means the first of the prophets to foresee the reconstitution of Yahwistic Hebraism in Palestine. Prophetic literature generally anticipates an eventually positive outcome of Yahweh's affair with Judah-Israel. We have already examined in Jeremiah and Ezekiel two of the more explicit expressions of that hope. On the eve of Jerusalem's destruction, Jeremiah suspended pronouncements of coming doom long enough to buy a parcel of ground and bury the deed for it in a jar for safekeeping — all as a sign of his sober confidence in the return of brighter days for Judah. Ezekiel, whose career embraced both siege and exile, envisioned in poetic fancy the reflowering of paradise from springs arising in a Temple-centered Hebrew theocracy. Yet in all of prophetic literature the lyrics found in Isa., chs. 40 to 45, the work of so-called Second Isaiah, are unmatched for their joyful anticipation of Israel's renaissance and their explicit announcement of the means whereby Yahweh's sovereignty over the nations will be exercised to that end.

Concerning Second Isaiah himself, we have little information — not even his proper name. His writing itself attests to his stature as a prophet of high culture and poetic imagination, and places him under the influence of the Isaianic tradition as one who wrote during the period of Persian expansion under the scepter of Cyrus (550–529 B.C.).

His poetry heralds an impendent and resplendent world event, and celebrates its arrival as a coming manifestation of Yahweh.

" And the glory of the Lord shall be revealed, and all flesh shall see it together." (Isa. 40:5.) The theophanous event, at first unidentified, is good news for Judah: " ' Behold your God! ' Behold, the Lord God comes with might, and his arm rules for him. . . . He will feed his flock like a shepherd." (Vs. 9-11.)

When finally he is ready to put his finger upon the human agent through whom the impending action is to be performed, the prophet names Cyrus as the coming Messiah of Yahweh: " Thus says the Lord to his messiah, to Cyrus " (Isa. 45:1). Even though the Persian conqueror does not so understand himself, yet the prophet argues that it is really Yahweh who has grasped the hand of Cyrus to subdue nations before him, to ungird the loins of kings, to smash doors of bronze and slice through bars of iron, to seek out treasures hoarded in darkness. Through current events Yahweh himself is speaking to Cyrus. " For the sake of my servant Jacob, and Israel, my chosen, I call you by your name, I surname you, though you do not know me. . . . I gird you, though you do not know me, that men may know, from the rising of the sun . . . , that there is none besides me; I am the Lord, and there is no other." (Vs. 1-6.)

What action of Cyrus is awaited, then, with bated breath? His overthrow of the Chaldean empire? A mere preliminary to the main event! When Cyrus has subjugated Chaldaic Babylon, he will next rebuild Jerusalem and repatriate the Jews exiled in Babylonia. The coming rehabilitation of Jews in their homeland will declare before all the world, history's concern for Israel, Yahweh's chosen! " I am the Lord, . . . who says of Cyrus, ' He is my shepherd, and he shall fulfil all my purpose '; saying of Jerusalem, ' She shall be built,' and of the temple, ' Your foundation shall be laid.' . . . ' He shall build my city and set my exiles free, not for price or reward,' says the Lord of hosts." (Isa. 44:24, 28; 45:13.)

The prophet, however, proceeds to the point of his proclamation by oblique reference, tantalizing digression, consummate indirection. He unwraps the content of his message by stages, disclosing first its general shape and only later its dramatic de-

tails. He stops the recital of his forecast to accredit himself, a
man of mortal flesh, as yet a messenger from Yahweh to Israel.
" All flesh is grass, and all its beauty is like the flower of the
field." Central importance attaches, therefore, not to himself, but
to the news he bears from the mouth of God. " The grass with-
ers, the flower fades; but the word of our God will stand for
ever." (Isa. 40:5-8.) He pauses in his proclamation to extol
Yahweh, its author, and to denigrate Yahweh's rivals — celebrating in majestic imagery the sovereignty of the former while
ridiculing in biting satire the impotence of the latter as agents
in cosmic and human affairs. (Vs. 12-26.) Even his forthright
naming of the coming messianic event and the new Messiah climaxes a series of hints, at once veiled and vivid, as to the identity of the man and his impending action. (Chs. 41:2-4; 43:5-7,
14-15; 44:24-28; 45:1-7, 13.)

Second Isaiah evokes anticipation and promotes understanding of the coming new thing by remembrance of things past.
Yet, like all the prophets of the eighth century and following,
his view of history is essentially eschatological and therefore fu-
turistic. That is to say, he understands the present, not in terms
of its beginnings, but basically in terms of its ending (*eschaton*),
its cataclysmic outcome as determined by the purpose and activity of Yahweh. He recites Israel's past, therefore, neither to
reconstitute and relive it, nor yet to argue for any basic intelligibility of human historical action as such. From his point of
view, the sum of human behavior would have no unifying thread
of purpose or meaning were not the capricious actions of men
reversed or canceled by the sovereign intervention of a Lord in
whose purpose there is no caprice. He evokes the past, therefore, in order to demonstrate that in every time the meaning of
Israel's current circumstance ever was and is to be found in the
impending cataclysmic action of Yahweh as announced by his
prophets. He turns to the past for archetypes of upheaval, for
symbols of the *eschaton*. By no means does he seek in history
prototypes of the logic of human behavior in history.

The historic exodus of Hebrews from Egypt, for example,

serves him as a favorite eschatological symbol. The memorable images of the Red Sea and of the wilderness experience provide proleptic participation in the impending messianic deliverance of the exiles from Babylonian captivity (Isa. 43:14-21; 48:20-21; 51:9-11; 52:11-12), a foretaste of Israel's existence in a resplendent new cosmos (ch. 41:17-20). In the very act of recalling the first exodus, therefore, he delivers the oracle: " Remember not the former things, nor consider the things of old. Behold, I am doing a new thing." Remember the old exodus from Egypt, is his counsel, only that you may trust Yahweh's word that he is about to enact a new exodus from Babylon. (Ch. 43:14-21.) He seeks acceptance of his message by arguing again and again that the prophets of Yahweh alone have been given foreknowledge of the startling outcome of major crises among the nations. (Chs. 41:21-24; 42:8-9, 17; 43:8-9; 44:6-8; 45:21-22; 46:8-11.) Even now Yahweh alone of all the gods is putting his sovereignty to the test of history by forecasting the astonishing benevolence of Cyrus toward the exiles and Israel. (Chs. 41:25-29; 44:24-28; 48:3-8.) Like his predecessors, Second Isaiah viewed himself as speaking a miraculously imparted word, and his message as itself the preliminary phase of Yahweh's emerging eschatological activity.

Parenthetically, it is one measure of our distance from the prophetic point of view that contemporary scholars tend to consider a prophetic message as at once a function of the prophet's imagination and of his cultural milieu. Our literary sources, however, often do not permit the reconstruction of the dynamic interplay between individual imagination and cultural situation. Whether Second Isaiah, for example, worked out in the style of Hebrew prophecy an actual forecast of political events in Iran, or whether he worked out his eschatology on the basis simply of the prophetic tradition and later incorporated an actually victorious Cyrus into his earlier expectations can no longer be known.[12]

In any case, the military occupation of Judah, the exile of her aristocracy, and the vacancy of her throne did not undermine

Second Isaiah's confidence in kingship mythology as the most fruitful model for the understanding of history. Modification of the model, yes. Abandonment, no! He is recognized among the most eloquent exponents of Yahweh's kingship. His theology, moreover, influenced a liturgical reform movement out of which came enthronement rituals celebrating the establishment of Yahweh himself, rather than of a human monarch, upon the throne of Israel.[13]

Yet his use of court mythology evidences no substantive change in the fundamental prophetic premise: namely, that the intelligibility of history is a function of the will and word of Yahweh. " His arm rules for him." (Isa. 40:10.) He sits enthroned above the vault of the sky, reducing men to grasshopper size, bringing princes and rulers of the earth to naught, nightly naming the stars into being, so that none is ever missing. (Vs. 21-26.) Yahweh himself is the King of Jacob (ch. 41:21) and of Israel (ch. 43:15), whom he has especially chosen (ch. 44:1; 45:4). Yet Israel's King and Redeemer is identically the Lord of the multitude of peoples. " I am the first and I am the last; besides me there is no god." (Ch. 44:6.) His dominion is over all: " To me every knee shall bow, every tongue shall swear " (ch. 45:23).

The central figure in Israel's past is Yahweh. " Who gave up Jacob to the spoiler, and Israel to the robbers? " To this rhetorical question the prophet replies: " Was it not the Lord, against whom we have sinned? " In short, the fury of foreign invasion conveyed the heat of Yahweh's anger, in spite of Israel's failure so to understand it. (Isa. 42:24-25.) The prophet portrays Yahweh's dealings with a people whose very existence is communal, and so also their guilt and retribution. " Your first father sinned, and your mediators transgressed against me. Therefore I profaned the princes of the sanctuary, I delivered Jacob to utter destruction and Israel to reviling." (Cf. ch. 43:22-28.) He pictures a radically different outcome of world history, had Israel only been obedient to her God. (Ch. 48:17-19.)

Yahweh's affair with Israel encloses the secret of world history — past, present, and future. " Truly, thou art a God who hidest thyself, O God of Israel." (Isa. 45:15.) So the prophet delivers as Yahweh's oracle to Babylon: " I was angry with my people, I profaned my heritage; I gave them into your hand, you showed them no mercy; on the aged you make your yoke exceedingly heavy. . . . Now therefore hear this, . . . disaster shall fall upon you, which you will not be able to expiate; and ruin shall come on you suddenly, of which you know nothing." (Ch. 47:6, 8, 11.) [14] Second Isaiah is the first of the prophets to characterize his message as " good news " (cf. ch. 40:9; 52:7), and the heart of that news is Yahweh's return to reign in Zion (ch. 52:7-10). " For a brief moment I forsook you, but with great compassion I will gather you." (Ch. 54:7.) Whoever may be his agents, Yahweh himself is bringing about Zion's deliverance (ch. 46:13) and the redemption of the Babylonian captives (ch. 48:20; 52:11-12). It is he who will make the enemies of Israel eat their own flesh, and be drunk with their own blood as with wine. " Then all flesh shall know that I am the Lord your Savior, and your Redeemer, the Mighty One of Jacob." (Ch. 49:26.)

Though Second Isaiah keeps Yahweh at the center of history, his casting of Cyrus in a messianic role evidences a basic shift in kingship symbology The beginnings of that shift appear already in Jeremiah, who identifies the king of Babylon as the servant of Yahweh. On Jeremiah's understanding, however, Nebuchadnezzar functions as an instrument solely of Yahweh's wrath — against Israel (Jer. 25:9; 27:7) and against Egypt (Jer. 43:10). The notion that powers hostile to Israel may serve the divine wrath has a long history in prophecy. (Cf. Amos, ch. 3; Isa. 10:1-16.) Second Isaiah's recognition of Cyrus as the crypto-messiah of Yahweh (Isa. 45:1), by contrast, legitimates a gentile ruler of a foreign empire as the agent of Yahweh's benign care for Israel. Cyrus is the royal shepherd of Israel. By him Jerusalem and the Temple are to be rebuilt (Isa. 44:28); by him the cup of staggering, the bowl of Yahweh's wrath, will be taken from Israel and placed in the hand of Jacob's tormentors (Isa. 51:17-23). This legitimation, without parallel in prophetic literature, frees Hebrew messianism to project its imperialistic dreams independently of a viable Hebrew political monarchy.

A still more fundamental shift in messianic symbology comes to view in Second Isaiah. Though he never explicitly calls Israel "Yahweh's messiah," still he repeatedly attributes messianic roles to Israel as a whole. On his view, what the monarch had been to all his subjects, Israel is now destined to be to all peoples. Israel effectively displaces the monarch as the vicegerent through whom Yahweh exercises universal sovereignty and maintains universal justice and peace. Though his status among the peoples is that of a worm, Israel will be made a threshing sledge to harvest the nations. (Isa. 41:14-16.) No mention is made of the monarch. Yahweh promises that the homage of nations will be offered to the people of Israel, rather than to the throne. Specified nations "shall come over to you and be yours . . . ; they shall come over in chains and bow down to you. They will make supplication to you, saying: ' God is with you only, and there is no other, no god besides him ' " (ch. 45:14). Kings shall serve as the guardians, queens as the nursing mothers, of ordinary Jewish children. " With their faces to the ground they shall bow down to you, and lick the dust of your feet." (Ch. 49:23.) [15] Speaking to Zion concerning her destroyers, the prophet delivers the oracle: " As I live, says the Lord, you shall put them all on as an ornament, you shall bind them on as a bride does." (V. 18.) Thus the fruits of national vengeance will adorn the people, not the monarch. Israel displaces the king as the one who shall be established in righteousness, prosperity, and secure peace. (Ch. 54:11-17.) Forecast is world government perpetuated, not through dynastic succession, but through Hebrew genetics (chs. 41:8-16; 54:3), a Palestinian Eden for the seed of Abraham (ch. 51:1-3). In his only reference to David, the prophet makes clear that the Hebrew people are heirs to the covenant of theocratic world imperialism. (Ch. 55:3-5.) Not a royal dynasty, but Israel himself is Yahweh's covenant of blessing to earth's peoples: " A light to the nations, to open the eyes that are blind, to bring out the prisoners from the dungeon, from the prison those who sit in darkness." (Ch. 42:6-7; cf. ch. 49:8-13.) [16] Yahweh will renew the world and reshape human history around Israel. (Chs. 41:17-20; 51:3.) In the dawning eschatological era, the mountains, the hills, the very trees of the new earthly paradise will celebrate an everlasting *pax Judaica*. (Ch. 55:12-13.)

The Servant Songs, comprising Isa. 42:1-4; 49:1-6; 50:4-11a; 52:13 to 53:12, offer provisional evidence of a third major shift in messianic symbology, depending upon the identity of the servant of Yahweh who figures centrally in them. Though Second Isaiah's authorship of the songs is no longer seriously challenged,[17] controversy continues to rage around the identity of the servant.[18]

Some of the evidence points to Israel as the servant. In one of the songs Yahweh forthrightly declares: " You are my servant, Israel, in whom I will be glorified." (Isa. 49:3.) The servant does appear here in the role of a prophet, but then the casting of Israel in that role is not limited to the songs. (Ch. 51:16.) Elsewhere than in the songs, moreover, Second Isaiah repeatedly specifies Israel-Jacob as the servant of Yahweh. (Chs. 41:8-9; 44.1-2, 21; 45:4; 48:20.) If in these controversial poems the servant always intends Israel — a debatable assumption — the prophet here advances a strikingly original explanation of the nation's time of troubles. Afflictions, elsewhere assessed as the punitive suffering of a guilty people (ch. 42:24-25), here are destined by Yahweh's impending redemption to become the vicarious suffering of an innocent Israel, wounded for the transgressions of his neighbors, chastised for their integration and healing (chs. 52:13 to 53:12). On these assumptions, the prophet directly answers the deep skepticism voiced in the complaint of his people against the injustice of their plight: " Why do you say, . . . ' My way is hid from the Lord, and my right is disregarded by my God '? " (ch. 40:27). The impending miracle of history, on this reading of the songs, is a people whose existence becomes prophetic, a redeemed Israel whose suffering

Yahweh will employ for the healing and renewal of all people. Ethnocentric, yes! But a far cry, this, from traditional accounts of national suffering, either in kingship mythology or in prevailing prophetic interpretation.

Some of the evidence suggests that the servant is an individual. In any case, Israel can scarcely be the one whose mission is to Israel. In Isa. 49:5-7, the servant appears as one destined from the womb to bring the remnant of Jacob and Israel back to Yahweh. This mission, as yet unaccomplished, is subsequently expanded to include all peoples. " It is too light a thing that you should be my servant [only] to raise up the tribes of Jacob and to restore the preserved of Israel; I will give you as a light to the nations, that my salvation may reach to the end of the earth." (Ch. 49:6.) Here the servant is portrayed as the mediator of Yahweh's coming salvation of Israel and of all mankind. He is one who is yet to come.

The evidence overwhelmingly suggests that the servant, viewed as an individual, will be a prophet, not a king. The coastlands are to wait for his teaching. (Isa. 42:4.) He calls upon the peoples to hearken; Yahweh has made his mouth like a sharp sword (ch. 49:1-2), has opened his ear, has given him the obedient " tongue of those who are taught," that he may sustain the weary with a word (ch. 50:4-5). Whoever fears the Lord obeys the voice of his servant. (V. 10.) A prophet, indeed, but a suffering prophet. (V. 6.) Despised and rejected by men, he is destined to bear our pain, endure our sickness, to be wounded for our transgressions, beaten for our reintegration and healing. (Ch. 53:3-5.) An innocent man, he shall bear the iniquities of many, that they may be accounted righteous. (V. 11.)

Moses, who also was called the servant of Yahweh, has long been suggested as the prototype of a prophet who suffers in life and is punished in death for the sins of his people.[19] The suggestion is the more appealing in view of the use that Second Isaiah makes of the whole exodus history in his eschatological prediction. From this perspective, the coming prophet is not Moses reincarnate, but another like Moses. Each is a prophet who suffers vicariously. As Moses in the exodus from Egypt, so the Suffering Servant in the impending new exodus mediates Yahweh's salvation, the former to Israel, the latter to all mankind.

The evidence examined suggests that the Servant of the Songs remains a fluid conception, signifying as the mediator of Yahweh's coming salvation, now a redeemed Israel, a people at once messianic and prophetic; and again, a coming prophet who is greater than Moses.[20] Clearly, Second Isaiah conceives the servant as belonging to a future already set in motion by the word he himself has heard and now declares from Yahweh. The coming servant and the coming theocratic domination of the earth by the Hebrews will constitute, moreover, not a political but a prophetic miracle.

Haggai and Zechariah. Time's perspective quickly diminished in Jewish eyes the stature of Cyrus the Persian. By neither Haggai nor Zechariah was he remembered as Yahweh's messiah. False was the apparent dawn in his time of the messianic age for Israel. Still, the prophetic hopes projected upon him were not entirely dashed. By formal decree (538 B.C.) Cyrus ordered the rebuilding of the Temple at Jerusalem, specified the overall dimensions of the project, authorized payment of its cost from the royal treasury, and remanded to the Temple its gold and silver vessels, long held as spoils of war in Babylon (Ezra 6:3-5). Yet under his administration actual work upon the Temple stopped with the laying of its footing. There is some doubt that he ever ordered the return of any Jewish exiles from Babylon.[21] Clearly his concern for the Temple and its cult did not commit his empire to Yahwism. The decree of 538 simply implemented in Judah his prevailing policy in religious affairs. The aim of that policy was to promote political stability by subsidizing and regulating indigenous cult practices within the numerous and widely diverse ethnic groups constituting the empire.[22] He was prepared to declare himself the agent of Yahweh or of any god whatsoever, so long as the service of the god suited his own imperial ends. A picayune messiah he turned out to be, when measured against the prophetic projections of Second Isaiah. Yet his management of Jewish affairs sufficiently fulfilled those projections for classic prophetism to survive a while longer as a credible mode of interpreting Hebrew-Jewish history.

The last daring projection of the politicotheological future was made by the prophets Haggai and Zechariah early in the reign of Darius I of Persia. The meaning and relevance of their forecast is effectively grasped only in the context of the Persian political situation then dominating the civilized world.

A ground swell of revolt, erupting while Cambyses II campaigned in Egypt, rumbled all across the empire when the emperor's hasty return to the capital was cut short by death in 522 B.C. Under his successor, Darius I, world upheaval worsened before it was eventually controlled. As one among countless measures aimed at restoring order, Darius appointed a Jewish exile of the Davidic royal line, Zerubbabel, the grandson of Jehoiachin, to be governor of the subprovince of Judah. Zerubbabel was accompanied on his return from Babylon by Joshua the high priest and a number of lesser priests and Levites. (Neh. 12:1.)

The prophets Haggai and Zechariah began their work independently, each in the second year of Darius I. (Hag. 1:1; Zech. 1:1.) Each was convinced that Yahweh himself foredoomed the efforts of Darius to check revolt and reweld his empire. Each counted political chaos as a phase of the world's end, destined to precede the messianic age.

Haggai spoke his first oracle on the first day of the sixth month in 520 B.C.[23] He addressed to Zerubbabel, Joshua the high priest, and all the remnant of the people, this word from Yahweh: " Poverty, inflation, drought, and famine are your lot because you have built houses for yourselves while mine lies in ruins. Rebuild my house that I may appear in my glory." Work was started again within the month. (Hag., ch. 1.) The stark new structure, far from fulfilling expectations, evoked nostalgia and grief for the splendor of the preexilic Temple. Yet the work

went on, impelled by a fanatic world's-end dream. In just a little while, the prophet predicted, Yahweh would again shake
heaven and earth, sea and dry land, the very nations themselves,
until this house was filled with treasures of all nations, until in
splendor it far outshone Solomon's. (Hag. 2:1-9.) He likewise
predicted a continuing domestic economic miracle, dating from
the laying of the first stone upon stone in the new Temple. (Vs.
15-19.)

By late summer of the same year, Darius had managed largely
to suppress the revolts against his throne. Still, Haggai's last
recorded oracle, on the twenty-fourth day of the ninth month,
confidently announced the imminent destruction of all alien powers by their armies locked in mutual combat, and Zerubbabel's
consequent survival as the sole political agent, " the signet
ring " of Yahweh's rule in the dawning messianic era. (Vs. 20-
23.)

Zechariah is generally conceded to have written only the first
eight chapters of the book which bears his name.[24] He began his
prophecies in the eighth month of 520 B.C. (Zech. 1:1), two
months later than Haggai, and ended them apparently in 518
B.C. (Zech. 7:1). His first oracle called for national repentance.
(Zech. 1:1-6.)

A subsequent series of visions portended the shattering of all
heathen power and the public identification of Judah as the medium in perpetuity of Yahweh's world dominion. (Zech. 1:7 to
6:15.) In the first vision, four heavenly horsemen patrolling the
earth symbolize the hidden sovereignty of Yahweh. (Zech.
1:7 f.) In another, the felling of four great horns by as many
smiths foretells a coming destruction around the compass of all
pagan peoples who had scattered Judah. (Vs. 18-21.) In a third,
an angelic land survey for rebuilding the walls of Jerusalem is
stopped by the word that Zion is to remain an open city, ringed
by Yahweh's protection alone as if by a wall of fire. The dispersed are summoned back to Zion to rule and plunder those
whom once they served in exile. (Zech. 2:1-9.) In a fourth vision, Joshua the high priest, surrogate of the people, " a brand

plucked from the fire " of exile, stands in filthy clothes before
the court of heaven to be accused by Satan.[25] Joshua is purged
of his iniquity, reclothed in clean apparel, given rule over the
Temple, and free access to deliberations in the court of heaven.
(Zech. 3:1-7.) Passing for the moment over the fifth vision, we
hear in the sixth of a flying scroll of judgment by which the land
is purged of thieves and perjurers — typifying all sinners.
(Zech. 5:1-4.) In the seventh, a woman's corpse, symbolizing
the putrescent sins of Judah, is delivered in a leaden-lidded cas-
ket to be enshrined in Babylon. (Vs. 5-11.) In the eighth, one
of the four heavenly charioteers patrolling all quadrants of the
earth reports the pacification of Persia on Yahweh's terms.
(Zech. 6:1-8.)

Zechariah himself interprets the obscure symbols of the fifth
vision: a lampstand between two olive trees — the stand holding
seven lamps, each having seven lips for flame. (Zech. 4:1-6a,
10b-14, 6b-10a.) [26] The lamps meant for him the all-seeing
eyes of Yahweh; the olive trees meant the two anointed who
stand by Yahweh as coagents of his earthly dominion. This sub-
stitution of dyarchy for monarchy as the historical form of Yahweh's kingdom on earth is without precedent in Hebrew prophecy.[27] Moreover, Zechariah's oracles clearly identify Joshua the
high priest and Zerubbabel as " the two anointed " — literally,
" two sons of oil " (Zech. 4:14) — who are the historic agents
of the divine sovereignty, one in the cultic, the other in the political sphere of the dawning messianic era. The oracle directly
conjoined to this vision, however, concerns the role of the Davidic heir. Yahweh himself will level before Zerubbabel the
mountainous obstacles opposing reconstruction of the Temple.
By the grace of God, the hands that laid its foundations shall
also place a capstone upon the finished structure. (Vs. 6b-
10a.)

The received text of a later oracle (Zech. 6:9-14) bears intrinsic evidence that Zechariah was involved in a plot to crown
Zerubbabel king. Two crowns were to be made from silver and
gold supplied by exiles in Babylon — one for Joshua, the other

for Zerubbabel, against the imminent day when Yahweh's secret dominion over all peoples would in these two men break forth openly before the eyes of the whole world. Connected with this plot is the prophet's forevision of a time then soon coming when the peoples even of strong nations would entreat Yahweh's favor, presumably placing themselves in the service of his two deputies: " In those days ten men from the nations of every tongue shall take hold of the robe of a Jew, saying, ' Let us go with you, for we have heard that God is with you.' " (Zech. 8:20-23.)

As the event turned out, Zerubbabel and Joshua never mounted, one the throne, the other the dais of Yahweh, to rule together as king and priest over all nations. Darius of Persia seems to have exploded this particular messianic dream, first by retaining his throne; second, by again stripping the Davidic line of political power; third, by bending Joshua the high priest to his own imperial ends. After the Zerubbabel messianic fiasco, later editors deleted his name from this oracle (Zech. 6:9-14). They did not bother, however, to remove from it clear evidence that Zechariah fantastically misread Zerubbabel's role in coming world events.[28]

The bizarre logic in this misreading of history is further manifest in Zechariah's stand on the Samaritan question. (Zech., ch. 7.) The Samaritans, remnant of old Northern Israel, for seventy years had fasted upon the anniversary of the destruction of Solomon's Temple. Now that it was being rebuilt, they sent a deputation to promote closer bonds with Judah in the common worship of Yahweh. Zechariah advised a blunt rejection, evidently because he regarded Samaritan worship as corrupt beyond purification. He seems to have shared Haggai's view that Jews bear holiness as an incommunicable gift, while Samaritan uncleanness pollutes by slightest contact (Hag. 2:10-14).

Clearly Zechariah, like Haggai, viewed the rebuilding of the Temple as a providential miracle raising the curtain upon a new eschatological era.[29] Thus he perpetuates the broad outlines of a Yahwistic theology of history. His work is distinguished from that of earlier prophets, however, by two significant emphases: (1) The archetypal events, in terms of which he predicts the future, he derives more directly and more consistently from his own imagination than from the antecedent history of Israel — the prototypical events occur in heaven rather than on earth.[30] (2) He tends to locate the meaning of history in Judah's relation to the law conceived, not as a dynamic expression of Yahweh's will for his people in specific historical situations, but as a fixed expression valid for all possible situations. Both emphases signal the displacement of the ancient Hebrew world view by a legalistic and sectarian Judaic religiosity. We are next concerned, therefore, with the transformations of messianic theology in early Judaism.

Chapter III

The Beginnings of Ecclesiastic Messianism

Back in the early days of the monarchy, priests were not far behind the prophets in making and unmaking kings. Along with Nathan, Zadok the priest played a central role in anointing Solomon to the throne of united Israel (I Kings 1:39, 45), and his son later served as the official priest in Solomon's court (I Kings 4:2). The priest Jehoiada plotted and personally supervised the assassination of Queen Athaliah, after first anointing the seven-year-old Joash to succeed her. (II Kings 11:4-16.) Yet for the period of the monarchy the priest is ideally pictured as the king's subordinate, whose role it was to " go in and out " before Yahweh's anointed. (I Sam. 2:35.)

In the period of the Second Temple (ca. 520 B.C. to A.D. 70), the priesthood — oldest of the Hebrew sacral offices — moved into the ascendancy. After the destruction of her independent statehood, Judah's control passed successively from Babylon to Persia, Macedonia, Egypt, Syria, and Rome. While these alien powers effectively suppressed the Davidic dynasty as a symbol of Jewish independence in the political sphere, they not uncommonly granted to Jews a subsidy for the Temple cultus and limited freedom in the religious sphere. In fact, from the time of Nehemiah (ca. 445 B.C.) until well within the next century, Judah existed under Persia as a semiautonomous priestly theocracy, even levying her own taxes and minting her own coinage. For the first time we hear the chief of the Jerusalem priesthood referred to as the " high priest." [1] The office of high priest, moreover, simply by virtue of prestige and power, fell heir to certain functions of the now defunct monarchy.[2] A shift of messianic hope from a royal to a priestly messiah awaited only the explosive pressure of persecution and the rising of a priest-hero. Harrassment and hero were both to be provided in the Maccabean period.

ASCENDANCY OF THE PRIESTHOOD IN THE PERSIAN PERIOD

The Chronicler. Author of I and II Chronicles, compiler and editor of the Ezra-Nehemiah complex,[3] the Chronicler provides a contemporary picture of Jewish life under Persia. The historical value of his editorial work is debatable, as is also the authenticity of the documents he incorporated into Ezra-Nehemiah, excepting Nehemiah's memoirs (mostly, Neh. 1:1 to 7:73a) — " the only undisputed source for Jewish history between 520– 175 B.C." [4] Yet unquestionably the Chronicler prolonged the influence of royal messianism in Judah by reshaping the history of Hebrew kingship to fit the fact that Judah was ending up closer to a priestly than to a kingly theocracy.

His reconstruction of the royalist tradition, the especial purpose in writing I and II Chronicles, depends directly upon the earlier literary work of the Deuteronomist.[5] Ostensibly he adopts from the latter a theology of history focused in Yahweh's covenant with David. (I Chron., ch. 17; II Chron. 13:3-12.) He places the Davidic dynasty upon the throne of Yahweh (I Chron. 29:23), Yahweh's kingdom in their hands (II Chron. 13:8). He paints of David an even more romantic portrait than did the Deuteronomist, who, for example, made at least euphemistic reference to David's part in the murder of Uriah. The defections of the Hebrew kings he details at great length throughout the Chronicles, and he specifies their unfaithfulness as the reason for the Babylonian captivity of Judah (I Chron. 9:1).

Yet by emphasis and subtle suggestion the Chronicler conveys quite another understanding of human affairs. His hopes center in Torah, Temple, and cultus rather than in the future of a currently discredited dynasty. While he pays due honor to David's political exploits, what evidently excites him is David's ceaseless care of the Ark, his gathering of wealth for construction of the Temple, his organizing and subsidizing of the Levites, notably the Levitical singers, of whom, presumably, the Chronicler himself was a member. He eulogizes Solomon especially for the splendor of the finished Temple, its appointments and services. Repeatedly, he celebrates the achievements of a Judean king as though the Davidic dynasty existed solely for its ancillary role in the Temple cultus.

Moreover, though he does not abandon the concept of Yahweh's dynamically direct involvement in the events of history (II Chron. 10:15; 18:31; 35:22), he is obviously moving toward a conception of Torah as an absolute precipitate of Yahweh's will in the form of commandments, statutes, ordinances — both ceremonial and ethical (I Chron. 10:13; 16:40; II Chron. 7:17-22; 24:16; 26:16-20; 27:2; 32:25; 33:8). It can be argued that the ultimate concerns of the Deuteronomist and the Chronicler come obliquely to light in the conclusions of their respective accounts of the monarchic era. Second Kings concludes in poignant celebration of politically inconsequential concessions made to an exiled king of Judah by his captor. Second Chronicles, in sharp contrast, concludes with the edict of Cyrus, which ends the " sabbath years of desolation " by proclaiming the return of the exiles and the rebuilding of the Temple.

The Chronicler's special interest in Davidic messianism grew out of a power struggle between Zadokites and Levites. In the Chronicler's time Zadokites were in power, the Levites out. The contest between these two priestly parties had its roots in the distant past. According to very ancient tradition, only a Levite could be a priest. (Judg., ch. 17.) [6] This custom seems still to have been taken for granted at the time of the Deuteronomic reforms under Josiah in 621 B.C., when legal steps were taken to purify the cultus by centralizing all worship at the royal shrine in Jerusalem. To avoid inequities otherwise attendant upon this reform, Deuteronomic law granted to all sons of Levi, including

Levites previously serving at provincial shrines, free access to the Temple altar and equal claims upon Temple offerings. The terms " priest " and " Levite " are used in this legislation interchangeably. (Deut. 18:1-8.)

Implementation of this law, virtually impossible by reason of the number of priests involved, was resisted from the outset by the Zadokite dynasty as an infringement of special Temple privileges which had been theirs since Solomon repaid his political debt to Zadok, the priest who aided him in gaining the throne.

Following Josiah's death, non-Zadokite priests themselves led a reaction against the Deuteronomic reforms, restoring the provincial shrines, renewing idolatrous practices there and even in Jerusalem. The Zadokite aristocracy largely escaped scathing criticism from Ezekiel and others for this corruption of the cultus, possibly because they furnished during the period of reaction a disproportionate number of priests in exile. Though Ezekiel regarded the Zadokites as stemming from Levi (Ezek. 44:15),[7] he distinguished Zadokites from Levites, and sought in his proposed cultic legislation to reduce the latter to an inferior status as Temple servants (vs. 10-14). In his usage, the term " priest," unqualified, means Zadokite as distinct from Levite. (Ezek. 45:4-5.)

The Chronicler simply assumed that a prevailing differentiation between Zadokite and Levite offices in his own day had originated in the time of David. He was aware of the tradition that until Solomon completed the Temple, priests had conducted sacrifices before the Tabernacle at Gibeon. (I Chron. 21:28-29; II Chron. 1:1-6.) But he knew also that the Ark had already been transferred to Jerusalem in David's time and settled there, thus ending Levitical responsibility for its safe transport. Most significant for his concerns was the fact that David himself had averted a potential Levitical identity crisis by recommissioning the Levites to sing continuous praise of Yahweh. (I Chron. 6:16-32; 16:1-6.) By sharply setting off the Levitical Ark tradition over against the Aaronite-Zadokite Tabernacle tradition, and by invoking the theology of messianic royalism, the Chronicler argued in effect that Levites and Zadokites of his own time had equally venerable legitimation and equal claims upon the Temple economy.[8]

Judah's internal situation during the Persian period was shaped by two returned exiles, Nehemiah and Ezra, of whose work the Chronicler preserved a record. For reasons no longer evident, the Chronicler placed Ezra in Jerusalem before Nehemiah. Mounting evidence suggests, however, that Nehemiah returned in 445 B.C., and that his work preceded that of Ezra.[9]

Nehemiah the eunuch, cupbearer to Artaxerxes I Longimanus, subtly exploited the intimate relationship of his high office to win from the Persian king a commission to rebuild the walls and gates of Jerusalem (Neh. 1:1 to 2:8), and a term appointment as governor of Judah (Neh. 5:14). He fulfilled his commission under incredible difficulties. Not the least of these was the stiff resistance offered by his fellow Hebrews in Samaria under the leadership of Sanballat and Tobiah (Neh. 4:7 ff.; 6:1 ff.), whose power was the greater as long as Jerusalem remained defenseless.

Nehemiah's governorship itself strongly influenced the social milieu within which messianic theology was destined to take new shapes. He provided for later generations a fortified Jerusalem — an incalculable asset to the Maccabean theocracy in their struggle for Jewish independence. He harbored against Samaritans, for their obstruction of his work, a contagious and implacable hostility (Neh. 13:7-8, 28) that haunted Jewish-Samaritan relationships for generations. He brought from the exilic community a passionate concern for Sabbath observance,[10] which he harshly imposed upon the city of Jerusalem (vs. 15-18); and an equally passionate hatred of intermarriage between Jews and aliens, which he ruthlessly opposed by means ranging from argument and curses to assault and battery (vs. 23-27).

Ezra, according to the Chronicler, was commissioned by the Persian king to administer, apparently in the whole of Palestine (Ezra 7:25), a Yahwistic code of law specified as the one then in Ezra's hand (v. 14). Under the terms of his commission, this sacral code became Persian law for the province (v. 26) and Ezra himself a " scribe of the law of the God of heaven " (v. 12) — a technical Aramaic title in this case, indicating his status as an officer of the Persian crown, and bearing as yet none of the connotations characterizing the term *sofer* in later Judaism.[11]

All this suggests that " the law of the God of heaven " was compiled by exiles in Babylon and its content approved by the Persian court prior to the granting of Ezra's commission. The code itself can no longer be positively identified. In the Persian era, though exactly when and how we no longer know, the Priestly Code (P) became the canon of praxis for the cult in Jerusalem; but available evidence for identifying P with Ezra's code, however tempting, remains inconclusive.[12] Our present Pentateuch, including as its latest stratum the Priestly Code, took final shape also in the Persian period, probably between 450–350 B.C. Yet that Ezra brought with him the whole of the Pentateuch as a binding Yahwistic-Persian code for Judah appears highly improbable, however widespread the notion.[13] It is more likely that Palestinian Priestly editors simply incorporated Ezra's law here and there within the Pentateuch.[14]

Though the source and content of Ezra's code is now uncertain, there is general agreement that its promulgation marks the beginnings of legalistic Judaism, in which a covenant of cultic law administered by a priestly dynasty displaces a covenant of state administered by a royal dynasty as the basic vehicle of Jewish existence under Yahweh.

The Priestly Code.[15] This code simply ignores the tradition of messianic kingship and presents the priestly office as the only institution mediating between Yahweh and his people [16] — a fact noteworthy in a document regulative of the cultus in the period. Further, P understands the covenant relationship as rooted in the believer's fulfillment of traditional demands and expectations. Earlier, the prophets, especially Jeremiah, Ezekiel, and Second Isaiah, had viewed the covenant relationship eschatologically; the Sinaitic and Davidic covenants, for example, only foreshadow an ever future and novel consummation of Yah-weh's dealings with Israel.[17] Thus prophecy locates God basically within the demands and possibilities arising out of the future and requires a critical attitude toward everything already exist-ing. Priestly theology, by contrast, locates God essentially within the demands and pressures for social conformity within the present.

Ben Sira. Like the Chronicler, Ben Sira honors the Davidic covenant; but he makes even more clearly evident a displace-ment of the Davidic line by the Zadokite priestly dynasty in the center of Jewish affairs. His praise of famous men (Sirach 44:1 to 51:21) [18] celebrates, perhaps more fully than fervently, the traditions of messianic royalism. He extols his favorite kings (ch. 47, *et passim*) and blames the downfall of Judah upon the lot of them, excepting only David, Hezekiah, and Josiah (ch. 49:4-7). He duly professes faith in the eventual fulfillment of the Davidic " covenant of kings " (ch. 47:11, 22), though he speaks of the Judean monarchy as actually ended (ch. 49:4).

Chiefly, however, he celebrates an everlasting priestly cov-enant established between Yahweh and all heirs of Aaron (Sirach 45.6-7), who himself was anointed by no less than Moses (v. 15) — royalists take note! He explicitly compares the Aaron-ite with the Davidic covenant (v. 25), and declares the renewal of the former between Yahweh and the descendants of Phinehas forever (v. 24), thus pushing the origins of the Temple aris-tocracy beyond Zadok to Aaron — Levites take note! [19] In the person of Simon the high priest, of whose public works and priestly splendor he seems to have been an awed eyewitness, Ben Sira saw the flowering of Judaism. The florid praise of his eulogy pictures Simon as the perfect priest and patriot, who has made the Temple a fortress, Jerusalem well-nigh impreg-nable, the court of the sanctuary glorious with his presence (ch. 50:1-21). Ben Sira's Simon, whether the first or second high priest of that name, is the strongest competitor among all the Zadokites for David's place in the affections of the people.

Had his successors lived up to his record, the Zadokite dynasty might have replaced the defunct Davidic house as the symbol of Yahweh's concern for Judah.

If Ben Sira wrote at the beginning of the second century B.C., as is commonly supposed,[20] his especial hero must be identified as Simon II, son of Jochanan,[21] whom later generations surnamed " the Just " (or " the Righteous "). Though the epithet honors the memory of the one priest, it marks the political and religious downfall of the Zadokite dynasty. Simon II (ca. 226–198 B.C.) received the title posthumously, because among the Zadokites he proved to be the last strong representative of the dynasty concerned for the strict observance of Jewish law and for the exclusion of all foreign influences from the cultus.[22] Zadokite corruption and incompetence were salient factors in the rise of the Maccabean dynasty to the high priest's office during the period of Judah's vassalage to the Greeks.

THE RISE AND FALL OF THE MACCABEAN PRIESTLY THEOCRACY

By courageously resisting Greek domination of Judah, the Hasmonaean (Maccabean) priesthood succeeded, where the Zadokite dynasty failed, in capturing the political and religious loyalties of the Jewish people. In the process, the Maccabees supplanted the Zadokites in the office of high priest and launched themselves upon dynastic adventures rivaling those of David. In trying to suppress the Maccabean guerrillas, the Greeks escalated the severity of measures taken indiscriminately against the civilian population. After such massive persecution, miscarriage of the Maccabean revolt itself precipitated, alongside the traditions of monarchic messianism stemming from David, the literature of an idealized priestly messianism for which the Maccabees served as the crude model. Jewish experiences in the Maccabean struggle underlie apocalyptic transformations of both these messianic traditions — the one kingly, the other priestly — as expressions of the hope and future shape of Jewish existence under Yahweh. The Hasmonaean revolt in turn is intelligible only in relation to a long contest among the world powers for control of the Eastern Mediterranean land mass.

In the early phase of the Mediterranean world contest, Persian campaigns to conquer the Greek city states twice aborted — first under Darius at Marathon (490 B.C.) and again under Xerxes at Salamis (480 B.C.). The residual threat of Persian power and ambition deflected Greek expansion eastward under the leadership of Philip of Macedon. In the preliminary stage of his countermove against Persia, Philip had successfully imposed his rule, by 338 B.C., upon the reluctant cities of Greece, all except Sparta. When he was assassinated, execution of his plans for war against Persia fell to his son and heir, Alexander the Great (336–323 B.C.). Success against Persia brought Alexander to the gates of Jerusalem, the surrender of which he accepted in 333. According to Josephus, Jaddua, last of the high priests mentioned in the Old Testament (Neh. 12:11, 22), was then still in office.

Alexander's amazingly swift subjugation of Persia, Syria, Palestine, and Egypt attests his military genius. His death in Babylon at the age of thirty-three left untested his power to achieve what seems to have been his larger purpose: a world community united upon the basis of Hellenistic culture. Yet he did precipitate a wide, if not a profound, diffusion of Greek influence, accounting for the fact that the language of the New Testament, for example, is Greek rather than Aramaic — the language of Persian diplomacy. Moreover, he founded in the Nile delta the city of Alexandria, later to become a most important center alike of Greek, Jewish, and Christian life and learning.

Civil war over succession to Alexander's throne eventually split his empire among three of his generals and the respective dynasties they founded. In the same year that he died, one of his personal bodyguard, Ptolemy (son of Lagus), seized full control of Egypt; by 320 he also held Palestine. In league with Ptolemy, Seleucus (Nicator) had established by 312 B.C. a measure of control over the rest of near Asia — the largest block of the empire. The latter made Antioch in Syria his capital. Antigonus Cyclops, operating out of Macedonia, was felled in the battle of Ipsus (301 B.C.) while still trying to make good his claim to be Alexander's sole successor. By that battle, the Antigonid dynasty was excluded from Asia.

For over a hundred years Palestine was exposed to the hazards of an inconclusive rivalry between the Seleucid and Ptolemaic dynasties. Repeated attempts by the Seleucids to expel the Ptolemies from Asia finally succeeded in 198 B.C., when Syrian troops under Antiochus III (223–187 B.C.) defeated Egyptian forces at Paneas. From that date until the coming of the Romans under Pompey in 63 B.C., Palestine was nominally if not always effectively under Seleucid control.

Sources for the history of the Hasmonaean period are several. I Maccabees, especially dependable, was written probably in Hebrew and in Palestine, about 130–100 B.C.,[23] from a Sadducean point of view favorable to the Hasmonaeans. The book forthrightly records events ranging from the accession of Antiochus IV Epiphanes in 175 B.C. (I Macc. 1:10) to the assassination of Simon Maccabeus in 134 B.C. (I Macc. 16:14). II Maccabees, a condensation in Greek by an Alexandrian Jew of an earlier work by Jason of Cyrene (II Macc. 2:23 ff.), exhibits a Pharisaic viewpoint and expresses concern for continued observance of the Maccabean festivals, possibly as a bond between Palestinian and Alexandrian Jews. Less dependable than I Maccabees, because burdened with legends of supernatural intervention, the book is yet a source for events from 175 B.C. to the defeat of Nicanor by Judas in 161 B.C. Jason's original work is placed around 130, the condensation around 70 B.C.[24] Josephus fills some gaps in the record.

Antiochus III dealt generously with Jerusalem: he resettled her refugees, freed Jewish slaves, rebuilt the city, restored the Temple, subsidized its cultus from state funds,[25] collected his tribute, and otherwise left the administration of Jewish internal affairs to the high priest, Onias III (198–175 B.C.), the Zadokite whom he had confirmed in office when he occupied the city. A like generosity (II Macc. 3:3) marked the policies of Antiochus' son and successor, Seleucus IV (187–175 B.C.).

In the time of Seleucus IV, however, a split developed within the Zadokite aristocracy between those who still opposed foreign influences upon the cultus and those who sought to accommodate Jewish life to the culture of their Hellenistic conquerors. Onias, leader of the traditionalists, tried in vain to match the achievements of his father and predecessor, Simon II, Ben Sira's hero, whose views he shared. A certain Simon, leader of the Hellenizing party, not only opposed tradition (II Macc. 3:4-21), but openly curried Syrian favor in an unsuccessful bid for appointment as high priest in place of Onias (II Macc. 4:1-6).

Under Antiochus Epiphanes (175–163 B.C.), who pressed ruthlessly for the Hellenization of Judah, Zadokite rivalry for the high priesthood and the conduct of the priests in office reached scandalous proportions. The high priest Jason (175–172 B.C.) openly paid Antiochus to remove Onias, his brother, from the office and to appoint himself instead. (Vs. 7-8.) He bought as well a concession to build a gymnasium near the Temple, secured permission to enroll Jews as citizens of Antioch, pressed for the adoption of Gentile customs until some of the priests were more active in the sports of the arena than in the service of the altar. (II Macc. 4:9-15; cf. I Macc. 1:11-15.)

Menelaus, a Benjamite interloper (II Macc. 4:23; 3:4) and the most perfidious of the high priests (172–163 B.C.), in his turn overthrew Jason by outbidding him for office (II Macc. 4:24), and then arranged the murder of Onias when the latter exposed him for theft of Temple vessels (v. 34).

Antiochus Epiphanes ([God] Manifest) in the meantime had invaded and pillaged Egypt (I Macc. 1:16-19). His cupidity unsated, he moved against Judah in 169, and personally invaded the sanctuary to plunder the Temple of all its gold and silver appointments and decor, of all its hidden treasure (vs. 20-24). Two years later he dispatched against Jerusalem his chief collector of tribute, who with a large armed escort sacked and burned the capital, demolished its walls, and erected at the heart of the ravaged city a massive citadel, the Acra, which he garrisoned with Syrian troops. (Vs. 29-35.)

According to II Macc. 5:1-14, this holocaust was precipitated by the deposed high priest Jason, who, believing rumors that Antiochus had died in his second Egyptian campaign, sought to drive Menelaus from office by force of arms. Whatever bearing strife over the Jewish high priesthood had upon the event, I Maccabees makes clear that the grim Antiochian measures were part of a larger plan to unify forcibly the Seleucid dominion on the basis of Hellenistic culture. (I Macc. 1:41-61.) To that end, Antiochus published throughout the empire a decree commanding the abandonment of indigenous religious customs, the profanation of ethnic priests and shrines, and the adoption of Hellenist gods and their cult practices. Breach of these provisions was punishable by death.

All Gentiles of the empire and many Jews complied at once — some gladly. But large numbers of Jews remained faithful to the Law, went underground, or hid in the wilderness. Antiochus appointed inspectors to enforce the decree town by town throughout Judah. Their procedure was simple. They assembled the townspeople and gave each person his choice: to take part in sacrifice to the Greek gods or die, then and there. Possession of the Jewish Scriptures, Sabbath observance, the practice of any conspicuous Jewish custom, were punished by death. Discovery of a circumcised infant brought death to his family and to the officiating priest. The boy himself would be hanged from his mother's neck.

On the fifteenth day of Kislev, 167 B.C., the Temple was desecrated, first by the erection of a pagan altar of burnt offering, and ten days later by idolatrous sacrifice. (I Macc. 1:54.) Soon the whole of Judah was hit by the pogrom.

In the same year, enforcement of apostasy was surprisingly blocked in the city of Modein by Mattathias, a priest in the line of Hasmon (hence Hasmonaean), a Levite family. In front of his assembled sons and fellow townsmen, Mattathias first boldly defied the king's decree. When promptly thereafter a fellow Jew stepped up to render the obeisance commanded, Mattathias sprang to the altar, killed both the Jew and the king's officer forcing the sacrifice, called for volunteers, and fled with his sons to the hills. (I Macc. 2:15-28.)

He and his friends were soon joined in the wilderness by a strong company of Hasidim (the Pious), members originally of a lay movement dedicated to strict observance of Jewish law, but numbering now many priests as well. Hasmonaeans and activists among the Hasidim organized an army and soon mounted against Syria a war of rebellion; against Hellenizing Jews, civil war. (Vs. 42-48.) When shortly the aged Mattathias died, his son, Judas, called Maccabeus, took command (166/5–160 B.C.).

Antiochus Epiphanes, his patience exhausted by this latest uprising, resolved upon a final solution of the Jewish question. He placed half his forces under his vice-regent, Lysias, with orders to destroy the Jews and parcel their land among aliens. With the other half, he himself set out for Persia to forage for funds. After three successive expeditionary forces had been chewed up by the guerrillas, Lysias called a halt to his end of the plan.

Judas pressed his advantage. He pinned down the Syrian forces in the Acra long enough to secure possession of the Temple and fortify it. On exactly the third anniversary of its profanation, December 25, 164 B.C., the Temple by his arrangement was cleansed and reconsecrated. The subsequent eight-day celebration was perpetuated as the annual festival of Hanukkah. (I Macc. 4:36-59.)

The heroic Maccabean struggle for Jewish independence had slight hope for success except for two circumstances. First, Syria's own independence was threatened from two sources: by the Egyptian Ptolemies, who even managed in 145 B.C. for three short days to occupy the Syrian throne (I Macc. 11:13-18), and especially by the Romans, to whom the Seleucids had paid tribute (II Macc. 8:10) since Antiochus III had led against them an ill-fated expedition in 189 B.C. (I Macc. 8:6-8). Judas astutely promoted a treaty of friendship with the Senate in Rome (vs. 17-32), which first Jonathan and later Simon renewed (I Macc. 12:1-4; 14:24, 40). The second factor favoring the revolt was a fatal weakness in the Seleucid dynasty itself. After Antiochus Epiphanes usurped the throne of his nephew, Demetrius, the dynasty was plagued by prolonged strife over possession or control of the throne until Pompey took over the empire in 64 B.C. and made it a Roman province. On numerous occasions this dissension directly aided the Maccabean cause. (I Macc. 6:17, 55-63; 10:6, 15-20, 67-89; 11:54-58; 13:31-40; 15:1-36.)

The Maccabees, on the other hand, were sorely handicapped by the defection of the high priesthood to the Syrian side after the time of Jason the Zadokite. During the Antiochian persecutions, the interloper Menelaus, prototype of all quislings, galled pious Jewish patriots more than the presence in their land of Syrian inquisitors. (II Macc. 5:15, 23.) His tenure of office came up for review when Antiochus Epiphanes, shaken by his reverses in Judah, died en route from Persia back to his capital. (I Macc. 6:1-17.) Menelaus hastened to the boy king, Antiochus V Eupator (163–161 B.C.), for reconfirmation of his appointment. But the young king, persuaded that Menelaus was a source of Syrian troubles in Judah, had him put to death instead. (II Macc. 13:3-8.) Antiochus Eupator himself was shortly to be assassinated by order of his cousin, Demetrius I (161–150 B.C.), who promptly appointed to the high priest's office an Aaronite named Alcimus. (I Macc. 7:1-9.)

Alcimus, with Bacchides and a Syrian army, entered Jerusalem pledging amnesty to the rebels. The Hasidim, victims of their own trust in the Aaronite priesthood, were among the first to sue for peace. When the city was in his control, Alcimus ignored his pledge and executed sixty Hasidim in a single day. Syrian reinforcements led by Nicanor could not stem the consequent fury of rebel vengeance. (I Macc. 7:26-50.) Yet in

160 B.C., Alcimus and Bacchides returned to Judah a second time at the head of Syrian forces, not only routing the rebels but felling Judas Maccabeus in battle as well. (I Macc. 9:1-21.) Alcimus succeeded in restoring briefly a legitimate Aaronite priestly theocracy. (Vs. 54-57.) But the efforts of the Temple aristocracy to Hellenize the cultus were doomed. Upon the death of Alcimus in 159 B.C., not only did the Zadokite-Aaronite aristocracy lose their lead in the affairs of Judah, but the high priest's office remained thereafter for seven years unoccupied.[26]

In spite of the strong Syrian garrison in Jerusalem, Jonathan, brother of Judas and his successor in Maccabean command (160–142 B.C.), had established by 157, de facto control over Judah. (I Macc. 9:57-73.) Thereafter he was actively courted by a succession of contenders for the Syrian crown.

Two years before he himself finally managed to wrest the Seleucid throne from Demetrius I, Alexander Balas (150–145 B.C.) made a bid for Jonathan's favor by appointing him to the high priesthood. Thus at the Feast of Tabernacles in 152 B.C., by appointment of a mere pretender, Jonathan became the first of the Hasmonaean high priests (I Macc. 10:1-21), and founder of the dynasty that supplanted the venerable Zadokite-Aaronite line. The Maccabean high priests, in spite of protests from the Pharisees, revived and adopted the title, " priest of the Most High God," [27] borne by the ancient order of Melchizedek in pre-Davidic times.

Jonathan's appointment was successively confirmed both by Demetrius II and the insurgent Antiochus — later the VI. (I Macc. 11:27, 57.) Yet Syrian dynastic struggles did not always favor him. By the treachery of Trypho, still another aspirant to Syrian power, he was taken hostage in 142 B.C. and subsequently slain. (I Macc. 12:39-48; 13:23.)

His brother Simon began his term in office (142–134 B.C.) under appointment from Demetrius II. Continuing civil strife between Demetrius and Trypho for control of Syria enabled him soon to achieve the semblance at least of Jewish independence. He gained release from tribute (I Macc. 13:37) and in 141 B.C. finally expelled the Syrian garrison from the Citadel (vs. 50 f.). He had, however, to repulse repeated efforts by the Seleucids to reestablish their hold on Judah. (I Macc. 15:25 to 16:10.)

Under Simon, Jewish gratitude and hope alike shifted from the Davidic strongly toward the Maccabean dynasty. Contracts and public documents were dated according to the number of his years in office (I Macc. 13:42; 14:27), as formerly they had been dated by the year of the king's reign. Though Simon was no king, the panegyric to him in I Macc. 14:4-15, portrays him as fulfilling the idealized image of Yahweh's messiah, the king in ancient Israel. His grateful countrymen erected on Mt. Zion bronze tablets commemorating Simon's achievements and those of his brothers, naming him high priest and ethnarch by choice of the people. (Vs. 27-45.) Yet the language of the commemorative tablet itself implies reservation as to the legitimacy of the Maccabean priestly dynasty: " The Jews and their priests decided that Simon should be their leader and high priest for ever, until a trustworthy prophet should arise " (v. 41). A priestly theocracy under a Maccabean dynasty was approved for the time being. Prophetic legitimation was reserved for the scion of David, the true hope of Israel, so potent still was the Davidic covenant as a politicoreligious symbol.

Simon was murdered, along with two of his sons, in Dok at a banquet arranged by his son-in-law, Ptolemy (I Macc. 16:11-17). His son John Hyrcanus, who barely escaped the same plot, succeeded him in office (134–104 B.C.). Hyrcanus, according to Josephus, was the only Jew ever to unite in his person the offices of ethnarch, high priest, and prophet.[28]

This grandson of Mattathias, however, was not content merely to consolidate the independence of Judah. After the death of Antiochus VII in 129 B.C., he marched against the cities of Syria; captured numerous towns east of the Jordan; subdued Samaria; razed its capital; demolished the temple on Mt. Gerizim (built around 330 B.C. as a rival to the one in

Jerusalem); overran and Judaized Idumaea; [29] pressed north to Scythopolis and west to Mt. Carmel by the sea.[30] All these conquests pointed toward a single goal, implicit in the Maccabean movement since the time of Judas: the founding of a monarchial dynasty, modeled after that of David, and controlling all territory within the ancient boundaries of united Israel.

But the times were not ripe for the Hasmonaean dream. The Yahwistic war cult of David's youth had been transformed into a Yahwism of Temple and the meticulous observance of law. Politics, then a theological art, was now desacralized; religion, then indistinguishable from statecraft, was now progressively desecularized. The Hebrews of Judah and Samaria, then united, were now long since the bitterest of enemies. Had Palestine been his, John Hyrcanus could have controlled it only by military force, and far too few were the volunteers eager to help him take it. Reputed to be the first Jewish ruler ever to hire foreign troops, he is said to have robbed the tomb of David to pay his mercenaries.[31] Smoldering resentment of his aims and methods burst finally into civil war, in which the rebels were promptly defeated.[32] The revolt may have reflected Pharisaic criticism of Hyrcanus, though the Pharisees as a group seem not to have been directly implicated in the uprising.[33]

Toward the end of his life, however, Hyrcanus came to an open break with the Pharisees,[34] politically the most powerful religious party of the period. By this breach he further jeopardized the stability of the Hasmonaean regime, whose shaky foundations had been exposed already by the murder of all heirs to Maccabean leadership except himself.

The Pharisees were one of three major and apparently new religious parties mentioned by Josephus as extant already in the time of Jonathan (160–142 B.C.); the other two were the Sadducees and the Essenes.[35] These groups seem to have emerged from the pressure of persecution and the ferment of revolution in the time of Judas Maccabeus (166–160 B.C.).[36] With differences of interpretation among themselves, all three were committed to the principle of Jewish religious freedom. There ended their intrinsic compatibility with Hasmonaean war aims.

The *Pharisaioi* (Separated), the occasion of whose separat-
ism is now unknown, observed strictly both the written Law
and its oral tradition, believed in the resurrection and final
judgment, expected Yahweh and the angels to resolve super-
naturally the absurdities of human history, tended to political
passivism except in defense of religious liberty, and had the support of the masses. The Pharisees seem to have been the direct
successors of the primitive Hasidim, many of whom fled to the
Judean wilderness at the beginning of mass persecution, some
of whom there made common cause with Mattathias against
Antiochus Epiphanes (I Macc. 1:29-48).

Sadducees, in contrast to the Pharisees, considered obliga-
tory only the laws found in Scripture; would have nothing to do
with resurrection or rewards and punishments hereafter; confessed belief in Yahweh's activity in history, but conducted the
affairs of this world as though human action were finally decisive.
They constituted a remnant of the lay and clerical aristocracy
of Jerusalem whose following was limited chiefly to the wealthy
minority.[37] They had marked Hellenizing tendencies and were
hated by the Pharisees. How the Sadducees were related to the
ancient Zadokites, other than in the etymology of their name,
is a matter of dispute.[38]

The name Essene, a Greek equivalent perhaps of Hasid (a
pious one),[39] probably applies to a number of rigoristic groups
splintered off the early Hasidim.[40] Their basic outlook was that
of the Pharisees, from whom they were distinguished by rigorous asceticism and their communal sharing of goods.

The anecdote advanced by Josephus [41] to explain the break
between the Pharisees and John Hyrcanus seems apocryphal;
the same story is applied in the Babylonian Talmud to Jannai,
one of his sons.[42] Yet the tale probably portrays the general
political scene with fair accuracy. The Pharisees not improbably
did brand the Maccabean high priests as impostors. An alliance
between Hyrcanus and the Sadducees is highly probable. They
alone could give his regime the stamp of legitimacy; he alone

offered the firm leadership without which their party was fragmented. In his swing toward the Sadducees, Hyrcanus seems to have gone so far as to abrogate certain Pharisaic legal innovations and to punish those who observed them.[43]

When Aristobulus I (104–103 B.C.) succeeded his father Hyrcanus in the high priesthood, he ensured possession of the office by murdering one brother and imprisoning two others. He was the first of the Hasmonaean high priests to assume the title of king.[44] When he died, his widow Alexandra released his brothers from prison. One of them, Jonathan — Jannai for short — she placed upon the throne, probably as her husband.[45]

Jannai ruled as Alexander Jannaeus, king and high priest from 103–78 B.C. Under his rule Maccabean territorial expansion reached its maximum extent.[46] In his person, on the other hand, the bankruptcy of the Hasmonaean revolution became clearly evident. Like Aristobulus, he murdered a brother to ensure his throne.[47] His insatiable lust for conquest repeatedly provoked Jewish rebellion, in which the Pharisees always figured prominently. The first revolt grew out of a riot against Alexander himself as he officiated at the Feast of Tabernacles in the Temple. Reckless in conquest, he was no less ruthless in suppressing rebellion, slaying six thousand fellow Jews in one revolt, fifty thousand in another. Pharisees were his especial target. He was the first of the Hasmonaean priest-kings to shed the blood of the " Pious." Had it not been for his mercenaries, he would have been unseated. His bitter subjects finally appealed to Demetrius III of Syria for aid against him. Demetrius won the ensuing battle, but fled the country when the Jewish rebels, who had invoked his aid, deserted in force to the banner of Alexander. This tardy shift of allegiance brought no amnesty. Alexander prolonged civil war until he had captured, imprisoned, and finally massacred in large number the leaders who dared to challenge his power.[48]

Jannai's widow and successor, Salome Alexandra (76–67 B.C.), by assiduously courting instead of persecuting the Pharisees, managed a comparatively peaceful reign.[49]

At her death, her two sons, Aristobulus II and Hyrcanus II, fought briefly for the throne. Aristobulus won; the brothers were reconciled. But then a wealthy Idumaean, Antipater, intervened to keep the contest going. By consummate intrigue, he induced Aretas III to supply and Hyrcanus to accept the support of Nabataean troops against his brother. Aristobulus was driven for refuge behind the walls of Jerusalem, to which Jewish troops under Hyrcanus laid siege with the support of an invading army. Both brothers sought the aid of Pompey, who briefly brought a measure of order. But strife was renewed. Pompey finally quelled the shameless contest only by laying siege to Jerusalem, defeating and exiling Aristobulus, naming Hyrcanus high priest, and organizing civil government under a representative aristocracy.[50] Thus ended the Maccabean theocracy and, until recent times, Jewish independence in Palestine.

Chapter IV

Apocalyptic Messianism

During the period of the Second Temple, apocalypse (revelation) displaced prophecy as the literary genre in which Jewish theologies of history found expression. The literary form itself was borrowed. Especially significant for the understanding of Jewish apocalypticism is the antecedent history in Egypt and Persia of the apocalyptic apocryphon (revelatory hidden [book]). Characteristically, such a work purported to have been written by a well-known figure of ancient times; set forth ostensibly future events, some of which were known to the reader as already having come to pass; and pretended that its revelatory content had been hidden from the public until the time should be ripe for its disclosure. The literary device itself presupposed that events occur according to predetermined plan, revealed occasionally by the gods or angels to men of their choice.

At a time when traditional Hebrew literature was being canonized as inspired Scripture, the pseudonymous Jewish author of an apocryphon secured by this artifice a cloak of authoritative antiquity. The literary form permitted him, at the same time, to use current popular impressions of historic events as a point of contact with his readers and a setting for his own message. The author and his reader alike were concerned in his reconstruction of the past, not for historical accuracy, but for symbolic insight into the meaning of their present situation. The language was often highly figurative. Kingdoms and individual rulers not favored by the author were sometimes portrayed as beasts or as lifeless statues. Well-favored kingdoms, sometimes also angels and even Yahweh himself, were portrayed in the likeness of men. Typically, the author dropped various hints as to the identity of persons and events depicted, though in numerous instances the meaning of his clues has been lost to us. Specific events, either portrayed or prefigured, belong to the traditions and times of the author, never to our own. The apocalyptic outlook was, of course, by no means confined to the true apocryphon.

Though Jewish apocalypticism was a borrowed literary form, its content was distinctively Hebraic and especially indebted to classical prophecy. Apocalyptic and prophetic theology concur in the belief that the purposes and actions of Yahweh are central to the meaning of human existence. They further agree that the eventual resolution of human affairs will find Hebrews the favorites of destiny, the privileged and burdened mediators of Yahweh's blessings to all peoples. Yet the two art forms differ profoundly in their presuppositions as to the manner of Yahweh's action. Prophecy sees Yahweh as responding in personal freedom to the course of spontaneous human behavior. Apocalypticism tends to suppose that he and we will follow a plan predetermined before the ages.

From influences of Persian thought, as well as from the experiences of exile in Babylon and persecution, first under Antiochus Epiphanes and subsequently under their late Maccabean heroes, apocalyptists derived a religioethical dualism that is lacking in prophecy. Between the creative intention of Yahweh and the actual performance of men in societies, the apocalyptist sees a chasm that Yahweh alone can bridge. (Secularized, his view might be expressed as follows: The actual gap between what man is essentially and what he becomes existentially is too wide to be closed except by an integrating factor that transcends both the individual person and the cultures he produces collectively.) Frequently, though by no means invariably, the present sorry state of the world is explained by invoking myths of the fallen watchers (angelic voyeurs) who lusted after the daughters of men. Further, the fascination of Hellenistic culture was often undercut for the Jewish reader by referring the origin of its technologies to those watchers. Thus the myths of the late Persian invaders became acceptable weapons against Seleucid efforts to Hellenize Palestine. The tendency was to see not only two sorts of angels but two kinds of men, two worlds, two ages — the one soon to be destroyed, the other coming into its own. The prophetic idea of recurrent eschatological judgment, confronting Israel in her this-worldly future under Yahweh, tends to escalate toward a final judgment ushering in an eternal kingdom in another world entirely. Apocalyptic thought almost invariably features belief in some sort of resurrection of the dead.

This résumé suggests the close relationship that actually existed between apocalypticism and Pharisaism. Not every Pharisee was an apocalyptist. Pious dedication to the law was wedded to no particular theology of history. Nor was all apocalypticism Pharisaic. Essenes seem to have held commonly an apocalyptic viewpoint. Neither was all apocalyptic literature messianic in outlook. Speculation as to the coming age could dwell simply upon the role of Yahweh himself, without attention to the mediating agents of his action. Yet apocalyptic messianism merits special attention, for within apocalypticism the technical meaning of the term " messiah " was transformed. Prior to that transformation, the " messiah " was simply a human agent, literally or figuratively " anointed " to carry out Yahweh's purposes toward Israel in this world, be he king, priest, prophet, Cyrus, or a coming scion of David. By apocalyptic conversion, the term came to signify the supernatural, preexistent agent by whom Yahweh would usher in his eternal kingdom in another world. The transformation was in large part the work of apocalyptically minded Pharisees.

APOCALYPTIC MESSIANISM AMONG THE PHARISEES

The Book of Daniel. A true apocalyptic apocryphon, this was the first great Jewish work of this kind and the only one to make its way into the canon of the Old Testament. The book comprises two collections, the first of stories (Dan., chs. 1 to 6), the second of visions (chs. 7 to 12). The author's interest in messiahs of any sort is no more than casual. Later messianists, however, by reading into the book meanings never intended by its author, have made it important to the history of messianic ideas. The unnamed author ascribes his work to Daniel, a character mentioned by Ezekiel in connection with the destruction of Jerusalem and the exile of the Jews.

Conveniently little is known about the actual Daniel, except his symbolic name, which means " God has given decision," and his reputation for rectitude and wisdom (Ezek. 14:14; 28:3).[1] The Daniel of our book, largely a creation of the author's imagination, figures as the hero of the stories and as the narrator of the visions. All the action occurs ostensibly in Babylon, where Daniel appears as a youthful Jewish exile in the service of the king. His exploits are set under Nebuchadnezzar, Belshazzar, Darius, and Cyrus; his visions under Belshazzar, Darius, and Cyrus; and he himself is supposed to have sealed the book (Dan. 12:4), until its revelations should begin to be fulfilled. Sixth-century Babylon provides only a frame for the author's message; Daniel, a literary device for its communication.[2] Neither the foreshortening of Babylonian history, nor incidental errors in detailing it, nor yet the incredibility of Daniel's exploits were of concern to the author or his intended readers.

The author does concern himself chiefly with the projected outcome and meaning of events recently occurring in his own day — events depicted in the visions as still centuries in the future " in the time of the end," where the author thinks he and his readers already stand. Firmest evidence as to the time of writing, the identity of the author, and the inherent thrust of his message is provided, therefore, in the historical details obliquely

supplied in Daniel's visionary "forecast" of events known to
the original reader as of recent occurrence. The visions offer
progressively more specific allusions to events in the author's
own time.

In the first vision (Dan. 7:2-14), four beasts arise from the
sea to dominate the earth: a lion, a bear, a four-headed leopard,
and an anomalous monster with iron teeth and ten horns, among
which emerges an eleventh little horn that quickly waxes large
and powerful. The fourth beast is slain, the remaining three ren-
dered powerless, and "one like a son of man" appears before
the Ancient of Days to receive an everlasting and indestructible
kingdom. An angelic interpreter focuses attention upon the
fourth beast, its ten horns, and little-big horn, who will persecute the saints of the Most High for yet three and a half years
until he is judged and destroyed by Yahweh, who will then deliver to his saints eternal dominion over earth's peoples. The
historical clues clearly suggest the Seleucid dynasty, ten of its
kings, and Antiochus Epiphanes.

The second vision, with the angel's interpretation (Dan. 8:2-
26), gives any slow-witted reader specific helps. The two-horned
ram is identified as the empire of the Medes and Persians. (V.
20.) The ram is overpowered by a unicorned he-goat, the Greek
empire. (V. 21.) The single horn of the goat is broken and replaced by four others, from one of which springs a little horn
that grows exceedingly large. With so much help, even the dul-
lard should recognize Alexander the Great, the Diadochi, and
Antiochus Epiphanes, who bans perpetual sacrifice to Yahweh,
overthrows his altar, and desecrates his sanctuary with alien
sacrifice (to Zeus), "the transgression that makes desolate."
Daniel overhears one angel declare to another that after 2,300
evenings and mornings, "the sanctuary shall be restored to its
rightful state" (v. 14). As for king little-big horn, he shall be
broken, but not by human hand.

In the third vision, "the man Gabriel [sic]" appears to interpret (Dan. 9:2, 20-27) Jeremiah's puzzling prediction that Jerusalem must endure desolation for seventy years (Jer. 25:11-

12; 29:10), a time span long since lapsed. Gabriel explains that each of Jeremiah's years stands for seven — a week of years. A total of 490 years must pass, therefore, after the fall of Jerusalem until the time of the end. "He" (Antiochus again) is the villain of the climactic seventieth week. (Dan. 9:27.)

The fourth vision details the history of empires from the fall of Persia to the imminent fall of Antiochus Epiphanes (Dan. 10:5 to 11:45). Numerous and quite explicit allusions are made to events occurring during the reign of Antiochus. (Dan. 11:5-45.) The vision ends with a prediction of an unprecedented "time of trouble" for the Jews, after which they will be delivered. Many dead will be raised, the righteous to everlasting life, the wicked to shame and everlasting contempt. (Dan. 12:1-3.) Clearly, the author supposes that the final judgment and the establishment of the eschatological kingdom of God are quite near — three and a half years away. (V. 7.)

The stories of Daniel's heroism in exile (Dan., chs. 1 to 6) may have been in circulation sometime before the visions were recorded. Various links between stories and visions suggest that they were written, if not by a common author, in any event with a common purpose of encouraging the Pious to be true to their faith in the time of the Antiochian persecutions.[3]

A variety of evidence, both internal and external, converges to suggest that The Book of Daniel was written in the time of Judas Maccabeus,[4] clearly after the Temple was desecrated by Antiochus and probably before it was reconsecrated under Judas — i.e., between 167–164 B.C.[5] The author's point of view identifies him with the Hasidim or their successors, the Pharisees. (Dan. 11:32 and elsewhere.) [6]

The unnamed author regards apocalyptic vision as a parallel of prophecy — both soon to be confirmed by the imminent action of Yahweh. (Dan. 9:24.) He incorporates as his own a prayer of confession imbued with a prophetic interpretation of Israel's suffering. (Vs. 3-19.) His picturing of history — as a succession of world empires finally superseded by the kingdom of God — fulfills for the first time the thrust of Hebrew prophetic

thought toward a universal theology of history.[7] At the same
time his thought bears the distinctive marks of apocalypticism.
In contrast to the prophets, he conceives of God as distant from
human affairs, working through his angels, some of whom may
even oppose his will. (Dan. 10:13, 20 f.; 12:1.) His dualistic
bifurcation of angels, men, and history expresses Pharisaic apocalypticism rather than prophecy,[8] as does his historical determinism (cf. Dan. 10:21). Central in his thought is the resurrection of the dead, conceived perhaps for the first time in expressly individualistic terms, surely for the first time as including the wicked along with the righteous of Israel.[9]

Mistaken is the view that The Book of Daniel predicts the
coming of an individual messiah through whom God will insti-
tute his universal and eternal kingdom on earth. The term " messiah " itself is only twice used, both times in the Apocalypse of
Weeks (Dan. 9:24-27), and both times in casual reference to
leading figures in antecedent Jewish history. First reference is to
the messiah in the time of Jerusalem's reconstruction (v. 25),
possibly Cyrus or Zerubbabel, more likely Joshua ben Jehoza-
dak, first of the high priests, Zerubbabel's peer in the reconstruction period, under whom the Yahwist cultus was reestablished.
Second reference is to a messiah murdered centuries later (v.
26), probably Onias III.[10]

The coming one " like a son of man " (i.e., like a man) (Dan.
7:13-14), to whom the Ancient of Days gives eternal dominion
over the peoples of the earth, is no individual, especially not
Jesus, but rather the final Jewish world empire. The figure of a
man, representing the empire of God's good people, parallels the
figures of four beasts, representing the empires of evil peoples
who suppress the Jews — as the author makes plain in his interpretation of the first vision. On this view, eschatological dominion belongs not to a dynasty or a man but to the Jewish saints.
(Vs. 15-27.)

In the story of the deliverance of Daniel and his two companions from the fiery furnace, the appearance of a fourth " like a
son of the gods " (KJV, " like the Son of God "; Dan. 3:25),

has again no reference to Jesus. The expression is simply a circumlocution for " angel," as the dialogue in v. 28 makes clear.

The Book of Enoch. R. H. Charles estimates that the influence of this book on the New Testament has been greater than that of all other apocryphal and pseudepigraphal books taken together.[11] Our present book comprises five sections, each basically an independent work: (I) chs. 1 to 36; (II) chs. 37 to 71, the Parables, sometimes called the messianic book; (III) chs. 72 to 82, a religiously biased calendaric study of the solar system, without special significance in the development of messianic ideas; (IV) chs. 83 to 90, an apocalyptic view of history distorted by pro-Maccabean myopia; (V) chs. 91 to 108, an apocalyptic diatribe *against* Sadducees and the Maccabees, especially influential upon the thought of Jesus as reflected in the Synoptic Gospels.[12] The structure is complicated by the interpolation of fragments from an earlier work, the Book of Noah, which constitutes in Sec. I, chs. 6 to 11; in II, chs. 54:7 to 55:2; 60; 65:1 to 69:25; and in Sec. V, chs. 106 to 107.

The several strata of the book, written over an extended period of time, represent a wide and sometimes conflicting variety of views on numerous subjects linked to the messianic interpretation of history.[13] A study of the sections oriented to their chronology will not only distinguish in them a radical transformation of Jewish messianic ideology, but will discern as well a close parallelism between the phases of that transformation and the changing theological estimates placed upon the Maccabean Priestly dynasty. Internal evidence identifies the authors of all sections as belonging to the Hasidim, or their successors, the Pharisees.

Enoch, sec. I, chs. 1 to 36, in substantially its present form, together with the whole of the Book of Noah, may well antedate the death of Judas Maccabeus (160 B.C.).[14] To convey his message, the author employs a naïve mixture of Persian mythology and prophetic theology of history. The myth of the fallen watchers he adapts to express his disdain of an alien culture — pre-

sumably Hellenistic. (Chs. 6 to 10; 12; 15.) " The whole earth
has been corrupted through the works that were taught by
Azâzêl: to him ascribe all sin." (Ch. 10:8.) History he views as
culminating in two catastrophic judgments. The first, by water
in the time of Noah (vs. 2-3), destroyed the mortal wives and
monstrous children of the lusting angels, who themselves were
then imprisoned in Sheol to await final judgment (vs. 4-6, 11 f.).
But the evil spirits of the slain half-gods who escaped their mor-
dant human flesh still prolong the earth curse. (Chs. 15:11 to
16:1; 19:1.) Coming, therefore, is the final judgment by fire,
into which will be cast the fallen watchers (ch. 10:6, 13), the
corrupt spirits of their slain progeny (chs. 10:15; 16:1), and
evil men whom they have influenced in every generation (ch.
10:14). In the meantime, the souls of the dead are consigned
to their respective compartments in Sheol until their final judgment (ch. 22:3-13), after which God's kingdom will be established on earth (chs. 10:17 to 11:2).

Earth shall then be cleansed of oppression, unrighteousness,
godlessness (chs. 10:20, 22), and the righteous of all nations
will adore God (v. 21). But quite temporal (ch. 5:7-9) and
earthy (chs. 10:17 to 11:2) is the paradisaic kingdom to which
the righteous, and they alone, are raised. The tree of life will be
transplanted in Jerusalem as food for the elect, and they shall
acquire patriarchal longevity from its fragrance. (Ch. 25:6.)
They shall live to beget thousands of children. (Ch. 10:17.)
Amid material abundance (chs. 10:18 f.; 11:1) they shall live
and die in truth and peace (ch. 5:9; 11:2). Excepting their piety and longevity, the resurrected saints are quite ordinary people. No hint is given as to the destiny of those who even in paradise eventually die of old age.

The author invokes no messiah to mediate the blessings of
this earthy paradise — located among seven peaks visible from
a vantage point somewhere in the northwest. (Chs. 24; 25.) God
himself will be the Eternal King, and the highest of the seven
mountains his throne, where he will sit " when He shall come
down to visit the earth with goodness " (ch. 25:3). This He-

braic view of God's nearness to the affairs of men is interrupted
only once. The account of Enoch's visit to heaven as an unsuccessful emissary of the fallen watchers (chs. 12 to 16) pictures
God as inaccessible alike to angels and men — excepting Enoch
(chs. 14; 15). The divine remoteness in this case, therefore, may
provide literary rather than theological accent, stressing the
sublimity of Enoch's vision.

Enoch, sec. IV, chs. 83 to 90, relates two dreams ascribed to
Enoch. The first is a rerun of the Noachian flood (chs. 83 to
84), when " heaven collapsed . . . and fell to the earth." The
second constitutes a scenic digest of what passes for Hebrew history from the time of Adam through the early Maccabean period to the last judgment and the founding of God's kingdom
on earth. (Chs. 85 to 90.) The scenarist, by his use of animal
figures to represent angels, people, and nations, produces a symbolic dualism — pious, pedestrian, and predictable. Herbivorous
cattle and sheep represent the Hebrews; carnivorous birds and
beasts, the Gentiles. Angels also are of two kinds: the good, represented as men, after the style of Daniel; the evil, as stars bes-
tialized (chs. 86:3 f.; 90:21) by their fall from heaven. A revision of the watchers' myth (ch. 86:1-6) thus provides a stylized
account of the ills to which mortal flesh is heir.

History reaches its climax after the return of the Jews from
exile. (Chs. 89:68 to 90:19.) Seventy faithless shepherds —
whose once obvious identity is now a matter of conjecture — [15]
have betrayed the sheep to their enemies, who pluck out their
eyes and tear the flesh from their bones. But in the fourth and
last phase of the postexilic era, horned lambs (the Maccabees)
arise from the flock. One becomes a great horned ram (Judas
Maccabeus), whom the ravens (Syrians) and their allies con-
tinually attack without success. (Ch. 90:9-12.) A sword is given
to the sheep (v. 19), who come to the aid of the embattled ram
in a final battle. God himself cleaves the earth with the rod of
his wrath; the carnivores among the sheep fall into the chasm
and are swallowed up in the earth. (V. 18.) The fallen watchers,
the shepherds, and the blinded sheep (apostate Jews) are con-

demned to the fiery abyss. (Vs. 20-27.) God himself rebuilds the sheepcote (Jerusalem), into which the dispersed and martyred sheep are gathered, along with the remnant birds and beasts, who now become their vassals. (Vs. 30, 33.) The eyes of all sheep are opened to the good. (V. 35.) The sword by which they delivered themselves they seal as a memorial to God. (V. 34.)

A horned white bull (the Messiah) is born to the flock; all flesh of field and air make their petitions to him (v. 37), and are themselves eventually changed into white bulls. At that time, the messianic leader becomes a lamb with great black horns. (V. 38.)

The author of these dreams clearly regards the Maccabean revolt as a prelude to an imminent and final battle by which the Jews will abolish war and establish the universal reign of God on earth — an apocalyptic view of history distorted by the myopia of a fanatic loyalty to the Maccabees. This ardent enthusiasm and his reference to a still warring Judas place his work before the latter's death.[16] His symbolic projections suggest that he expected the consummation around 140–130 B.C.

The gathering of men and angels before the judgment throne of God, he locates, not in the mountains of the northwest as in Sec. I, but in Palestine. (Vs. 20 f.) He centers the coming paradise, not in Jerusalem and a purified earth, but in a New Jerusalem, built by God. (Vs. 28-29, 33.) He envisions paradise, not as an earthy utopia, but as a spiritual state — a revival of Yahwism. (Vs. 35, 38.) The resurrection of martyred Jews he takes for granted (v. 33), but the precise character of the resurrection is of no concern to him. Unlike his predecessor, he revives expectations of a coming Messiah, who arises, however, from the community itself, a man among men, whether a priest-king or a scion of David he does not speculate. (Vs. 37-38.) The Messiah is to be God's agent in the coming spiritual transformation of those who squeak through the last judgment. Thus in many ways he prolongs the prophetic vision of history oriented to Israel's future under God on this earth. Judas Maccabeus is simply the agent through which that future breaks in.

Enoch, sec. V in part, chs. 91 to 104, in its original elements,[17] is an apocalyptic diatribe produced in the heat of partisan religious strife. The author identifies himself with a purist party (ch. 97:4), designated as the righteous (chs. 91:12; 94:3; 95:7; 97:1), the wise (ch. 98:9), the children of heaven (ch. 100:1), who uphold the law against apostate and idolatrous opponents (ch. 99:2, 14), and who affirm God's knowledge of sin (ch. 98:6), divine judgment (ch. 91:15), and the resurrection of the righteous (ch. 92:3). He bitterly opposes another party, designated as sinners and godless (chs. 91:12; 94:11; 95:7), the foolish (ch. 98:9), the children of earth (ch. 102:3), who have perverted (ch. 94:10) and forsaken the law (ch. 98:9), who trust in their own riches (ch. 97:8-9), who oppress and persecute the righteous (ch. 103:11-12), who deny divine retribution (ch. 104:7) and scoff at the idea of resurrection (ch. 102:6-8). At the time of writing, Jewish rulers are allied with the antinomian party and implicated with them in robbing and murdering the Pious (chs. 103:14-15; 104:3).

This configuration of events has its historical counterpart only in the opposition between Sadducees and Pharisees after the break between the latter and John Hyrcanus (ca. 109 B.C.). Depending upon the weight given the charge that rulers are implicated in the murder of the Pious, the situation may well be that of Pharisaic persecution under Alexander Jannaeus or Aristobulus II.[18] The author would seem, therefore, to have been a Pharisee writing between 95–76 B.C. or between 73–67 B.C.

This author appropriates the apocalyptic schema of an earlier work, the Apocalypse of Weeks. The latter envisions history in ten periods (weeks), seven of them already past, three yet to come. The first seven culminated respectively in the birth of Enoch; Noah's escape from the flood; the call of Abraham; the delivery of the law at Sinai; the building of the Temple; apostasy, destruction of the Temple, and exile; postexilic apostasy. (Ch. 93:10.) In the eighth period, sinners will be delivered to the sword of the righteous whom they have persecuted. (Ch. 91:12.)

In the ninth week, the judgment of the righteous will be executed upon the nations (v. 14); at the close of the tenth, the great final judgment will bring even the watchers to divine retribution (v. 15). Thereupon heaven and earth will be destroyed and a new heaven created for unending weeks of sinless righteousness forever. (Vs. 16-17.)

The author's imagination struggles with the implications of two catastrophic failures: first, that of Hebrew monarchy; second, that of the Maccabean priest-kings. The Maccabean rulers he dismisses with bitter references to their part in the persecution of the righteous; the Maccabees are allied with the enemy. (Chs. 103:14-15; 104:3.) He expresses no faith whatever in messiahs, past or future.[19] Though he adapts the watchers myths to his understanding of the world's evil, he is dimly aware that they project an essentially human condition. Sin has not actually been sent upon earth; man has created it (ch. 98:4) and is himself responsible for the sorry state of world affairs. Still, the writer has not abandoned quite all hope that men in their secular pursuits can realize, however ignobly, some immanent good. God's kingdom, for a little while, will yet be manifest upon this present earth. (Ch. 91:12 14.) Apostasy and violence must first greatly increase (vs. 5-7) before Yahweh's reign on earth begins. The sword will herald its coming: not, however, the sword of Jewish national freedom wielded by Maccabeans against the Gentiles (as in chs. 83 to 90), but the sword of divine judgment wielded against sinners by the righteous. Sin for this author is not a universal condition of private and public manhood against which every man must struggle. He views sin and evil in terms partisan and partly paranoid: we who are righteous find pitted against us all the others. The Maccabean nationalist of chs. 83 to 90, for whom Gentiles are the enemy, makes place in New Jerusalem for those who convert to Judaism and serve the Jews. But this persecuted Pharisee sees neither redemption nor any place at all for Sadducees in God's coming earthly kingdom. Sinners and their allies are destined to be wiped out of existence by intestine strife (ch. 100:1-3), or by the sword of the righteous (chs. 91:12; 96:1, 6, 8; 99:6, 9, 16). The righteous alone will survive to enjoy the healing, prosperity, and rest of God's reign on earth. (Chs. 91:13; 96:3-8.)

This apocalyptic picture, however, is no manifesto of revolution to usher in Utopia. The author is no activist. He has no more than casual interest in the coming of the kingdom of God on earth. His deepest hopes project beyond history, beyond this world, beyond any present heaven. He awaits the final judgment, the destruction alike of heaven and earth. (Ch. 91:15-16.) At that time the spirits of the unrighteous will be cast forever into the fiery darkness of Sheol.[20] (Chs. 99:11; 103:7-8.) From other parts of Sheol the righteous dead (ch. 102:5, 11), their long sleep guarded by angels (ch. 100:5), will be raised as pure spirits to life everlasting (ch. 103:3-4). Unlike the naïve author of chs. 1 to 36, or the devoted nationalist of chs. 83 to 90, this Pharisee affirms no resurrection of the body. He places the scene of final beatitude neither on earth (chs. 1 to 36), nor yet in the New Jerusalem of God's building (chs. 83 to 90). For him, the coming of God's kingdom on earth only preludes its consummation in heaven — a new and uncorrupted heaven (ch. 91:16) which has now no earthly counterpart. For the righteous alone will the portals of heaven open. (Ch. 104:2.) There their joy will be celestial (v. 4), their companions the angels (v. 6).

Enoch, sec. II, chs. 37 to 71, the Parables of Enoch, by reason of their exceptional originality, strongly reflect the milieu out of which New Testament messianism arose.[21] Here for the first time in Jewish literature we encounter the idea of a preexistent heavenly being (chs. 46:1; 48:3, 6; 62:7), seated on God's throne (chs. 51:3; 62:2) in heaven (chs. 39:6; 71:14), now hidden in the Lord, but already revealed to his saints (chs. 48:7; 62:7) as the one who is coming in judgment and glory to reign over the earth. In him dwells the righteousness of God (ch. 71:14), the spirit of wisdom, insight, understanding, and might (ch. 49:3). He knows the secrets of men, and in his presence none can utter a lying word. (V. 4.) When he comes, earth, Sheol, and hell will give up their dead. (Ch. 51:1-2; cf. ch.

62:15.) He will judge angels (chs. 61:8; 55:4) and men (ch. 38:3), both the righteous (chs. 45:3; 62:3) and sinners, whom he will slay with the word of his mouth (ch. 62:2). He will break the teeth of sinners (ch. 46:4) and cause them to be banished from the face of the earth and destroyed forever (chs. 53:2; 69:27), enchained in a place of destruction (ch. 69:28). The fallen angels, now chained and tortured, " on that great day " will be cast into the fiery furnace. (Ch. 54:6.) The spirit of the righteous dead abide in him (ch. 49:3) until the final resurrection and judgment. He will destroy the kingdoms of this world (chs. 46:4; 52:6) and reign over the righteous in a transformed heaven and earth (ch. 45:3-6). He himself will save the righteous (chs. 48:7; 49:3; 51:2) and will eat, lie down, and rise up with them forever (ch. 62:14; cf. ch. 71:16); for they, too, shall then have eternal life, life unending, days without number (ch. 58:3). They will have mansions in heaven (ch. 42:2), and will be clothed in garments of life and glory — clothing that never grows old (ch. 62:16). They will walk forever in the ways of the Righteous One and never be separated from him forever and ever (ch. 71:16).

Four titles already current in Jewish literature are here transformed by their application to this preexistent being. The technical meaning of the term " messiah " (*christos*) here undergoes radical transformation. The term previously designated any *human* agent through whom God blesses Israel, be he king, priest, Cyrus, or a future heir in the dynastic succession. *Christos* here specifies the unique *heavenly* agent of God's coming kingdom. (Chs. 48:10; 52:4.) The " righteous [man] " (*tsaddiq = dikaios*), a descriptive name often applied to men in the Old Testament (Deut. 16:19; Isa. 57:1; Ezek. 3:21; Hab. 2:4), becomes here a specific title of the Righteous One who is the heavenly prototype of all human righteousness (Enoch 38:2; 53:6). Many people of Old Testament times were called God's elect or chosen (*bachir*): Moses (Ps. 106:23), David (Ps. 89:3), Israel (Isa. 45:4), the " servant " (Isa. 42:1), God's people (Isa. 43:20); but the equivalent term here functions as a proper

name for the expected heavenly deliverer, the Elect One (Enoch
40:5; 45:3; 49:2, 4; 51:3, 5; 52:6, 9; 53:6; 55:4; 61:5, 8, 10;
62:1). Daniel's metaphor for triumphant Israel, " one like a son
of man " (Dan. 7:13-14), here names a celestial individual the
Son of Man (Enoch 46:2-4; 48:2; 62:5, 7, 9, 14; 63:11; 69:26,
27, 29; 70:1; 71:14, 17), who will have everlasting dominion
after the final judgment. All four titles, referring to an expected
hominoid from heaven, are applied with similar meaning to Jesus in the New Testament.[22]

Parenthetically, we are also here introduced for the first time
in Jewish literature to the angels of punishment (Enoch 53:3)
and to the further idea that the first defection of the fallen angels
was their voluntary subjection to Satan (ch. 54:6).

The bitter hostility expressed in the Parables toward " the
kings and the mighty " not only provides clues to the situation
in which the Parables were written, but suggests as well the reasons for this radical shift of messianic expectations away from
all human deliverers toward a suprahistorical heavenly savior of
the righteous.

Significantly, references to " the kings and the mighty "
clearly identify groups within the Jewish community. These are
the unrighteous, who trust in their riches and put their faith in
the " gods " produced by their own hands. (Ch. 46:7.) Just as
Gentile rulers look to gold and silver for salvation and depend
for security upon martial iron and breastplates of bronze (ch.
52:7-9), so " the kings and the mighty " place their hope, not
in the Son of Man, but in the symbols of worldly power (ch.
63:7). They do not acknowledge their power as deriving from
God (ch. 46:5); in fact, they have denied the Lord and his Messiah (ch. 48:10). They reject the very idea of heaven. (Ch.
45:1.) They have oppressed God's children (ch. 62:11), have
persecuted the synagogues and the faithful who depend upon the
Lord (ch. 46:8). They have slain the saints until the prayers of
the righteous and the blood of their martyrs cry out for God's
vengeance. (Ch. 47:1-2.)

But one day the kings and the mighty will stand to see the

righteous judged by the Son of Man. Terrified, they will recognize him. (Ch. 62:3-5.) Though now they possess the earth (chs. 48:8; 62:6; 63:12) and rule it (ch. 62:9), they will then fall to their faces before him and plead for mercy at his hand (ch. 62:9). But he will unseat them and strip them of their power, because on this earth they did not extol and praise him. (Ch. 56:4-5.) He will deliver them into the hands of the elect (ch. 48:9) and finally turn them over to the angels of punishment (chs. 62:11; 63:1), to provide a spectacle of vengeance delightful for the righteous; his sword will be drunk with their blood (ch. 62:11-12). Too late they will worship the Lord of Spirits and his Messiah (chs. 63:4 f.; 62:6); yet even they will confess the justice of his judgment which consigns to Sheol both themselves and the unrighteous gain in which they trusted (ch. 63:8-10).

The " mighty " are evidently the Sadducees. The " kings " can be none other than the late Maccabean priest-kings, who persecuted the majority party of their own people, for the Romans are not mentioned, and the Sadducees, though allied with the late Maccabees, were hostile to the rulers appointed by Rome. The alliance of Sadducees with the rulers of Judah in persecution of Pharisees reflects the reign of Alexander Jannaeus (103–76 B.C.) or of Aristobulus II (66–63 B.C.). The reign of Salome Alexandra (76–67 B.C.) is excluded, for she strongly supported the Pharisaic party. The evidence suggests that the Parables were written between 103–76 or between 66–64 B.C., surely not after 63 B.C. when Pompey assumed control of Palestine.

Further, the Parables clearly repudiate the Hasmonaean priest-kings, who not only had aborted the original aims of the Maccabean revolt, but had turned its force against the majority of the Jewish people. The cosmic dualism of the Parables constitutes, in fact, the abandonment of all hope that the promise of the future will be realized through human instrumentalities at all. The Messiah, though manlike, is no mortal. Without beginning or end, he comes down from heaven to reverse the processes of history by segregating good and evil, destroying the latter and so transforming heaven and earth alike.

The fact that the author(s) couches what he has to say in parabolic form raises the tantalizing possibility that he does not always intend to be taken literally. Does, for example, his personification of Wisdom and Unrighteousness, in ch. 42:1-3, exhibit the gap between the purely humane possibilities latent within men, on the one hand, and the distortedly destructive realization of those possibilities in the concrete decisions of life, on the other? Does his mythology of light and darkness (chs. 39:2, 4; 45:4; 46:6; 58:3; 63:6), and do his angels and demons alike extrapolate dimensions of specifically human experience? When he portrays the righteous as hating and despising " this world " (ch. 48:7), and when he effectively bids them hope for the peace that proceeds from " the world to come " (ch. 71:15), does he thereby express confidence in the prohuman potential within man to overcome his antihumanity as expressed in social and interpersonal existence?

Traditional scholarship has discerned no such subtle intention in the author's use of the parable as a literary form.[23] Further, the author's imagination seems captive to the idea that God is literally a self-existent super-Person. That presupposition itself becomes an ultimate literary frame, inviting the author and his reader alike to the credulous assumption that the three basic parables (chs. 38 to 44; 45 to 57; 58 to 69) report privileged communications from God to the author in person.

Interpretation of the Parables is further complicated by their apparent dependence upon at least two other Pharisaic documents: a " Son of Man " source and an " Elect One " source, possibly of independent authorship. Final discrimination of the two sources awaits recovery of the original Greek version.[24] Provisional analysis suggests that the portraits of the coming Messiah in the two sources reduplicate each other except in two significant details: (1) the Son of Man source alone ascribes preexistence to the Messiah; (2) the Elect One source alone specifies the tribulations that will afflict the Jews before the last judgment (ch. 56), deals with the conversion of neutral Gentiles (ch. 50:2-4), and details the return of dispersed Jews to Palestine (ch. 57). Both sources retain traces of the idea of a premessianic war in which the righteous will be vindicated by the sword. The Son of Man source places the sword in God's hand (ch. 62:12); the Elect One source leaves it in the eager hands of the righteous (chs. 38:5; 48:9-10; 50:2). In these several respects the two sources remain unreconciled. They share the dominant theme of a sudden appearance of the Messiah and the catastrophic resurrection and judgment of the dead.

The Testaments of the Twelve Patriarchs. This work purports to preserve the last will and testament of Jacob's sons, each to his respective heirs. Typically, each presents embellished stories (Halakah) concerning the patriarch's exploits, followed by ethical injunctions to his children, and concluding with apocalyptic predictions concerning the Messiah or the final Messianic Kingdom. The text is extant in a number of versions, of which the Greek is demonstrably a translation from lost Hebrew original(s).[25] A late Hebrew Testament of Naphtali differs not only from the Greek text, but also from a Hebrew fragment of the same title found at Qumran.[26] This difference and the absence at Qumran of any text representing the collected testaments, argues against Essene authorship of the present book.

Charles views all twelve of the testaments as the work of a single author, a Pharisee, who recognized only a Levitical priest-king as the Messiah. In support of this view he adduces numerous passages: Testaments of Levi 8:14; 18; Judah 24:1-3; Dan 5:10-11; Joseph 19:5-9; but principally Reuben 6:7-12.[27] The latter passage clearly represents a transfer of hope from a Davidic to a Levitical messianic dynasty:

> For to Levi God gave the sovereignty. . . . Therefore I command you to hearken to Levi, because he shall know the law of the Lord, and shall give ordinances for judgement and shall sacrifice for all Israel until the consummation of the times, as the anointed High Priest, of whom the Lord spake. . . . And draw ye near to Levi in humbleness of heart, that ye may re-

ceive a blessing from his mouth. For he shall bless Israel and
Judah, because him hath the Lord chosen to be king over all
the nation. And bow down before his seed, for on our behalf
it will die in wars visible and invisible, and will be among you
an eternal king.

Charles identifies this dynasty of priest-kings as Hasmonaean.
He argues that reference to the establishment of a new priesthood by a " new name " (T. Levi 8:14) specifies the Maccabees, who were the first Jewish priests to assume the title
" priests of the Most High God," anciently borne by the Canaanitic priest-king Melchizedek (Gen. 14:18). On the basis of
the next verse (T. Levi 8:15), Charles further argues that the
founder of this royal-priestly dynasty could have been none
other than John Hyrcanus, who alone of all the Hasmonaean
priest-kings was considered also a prophet.[28] He infers accordingly that the Testament of Levi, ch. 18:2-14, is a messianic
hymn composed in honor of John Hyrcanus.[29] On the further
assumption that Levi 6:11 most probably refers to the destruction of Samaria by Hyrcanus, he pinpoints the writing of the
book as a whole between 109–107 B.C.[30]

References to a messiah in the succession of Judah (i.e., a
Davidic messiah) Charles regards as interpolations made between 70–40 B.C. by Pharisees disillusioned by the lewdness and
venality of Alexander Jannaeus and Aristobulus II. Besides
these and other Jewish additions to the text, all aimed at the
overthrow of the Maccabees,[31] he sees also numerous additions to it by Christians who sought to enforce their interpretation of the book as a prediction of the coming of Jesus as the
Christ.[32]

The Qumran finds have reopened to scholarly debate numerous conclusions drawn by Charles.[33] It now seems that the original work was possibly no more than a single testament, that
the completed twelve are the work of several authors, and that
several of the testaments were condensed and revised by various
redactors. Though Essene origin is improbable, numerous parallels between Essene and New Testament messianism [34] evidence

the pre-Christian currency of ideas formerly regarded as New Testament innovations. Such evidence complicates the current debate, not as to the fact, but as to the extent, of Christian influences upon the collected testaments in their final form.

By no means conclusive is the evidence for identifying the Maccabean priest-kings with the Levitical royal dynasty of the testaments. The Essenes, we now know, regarded the Hasmonaean high priests as impostors, and expected a restoration of the Zadokite dynasty in the messianic age. Aside from that fact, reference to a new priesthood, bearing a new name (T. Levi 8:14), could point to the Zadok of Solomon's time rather than, as Charles supposed, inevitably to the Maccabees.[35] Neither is there sufficient reason for viewing the messianic hymn in the Testament of Levi (ch. 18:2-14) as written in honor of John Hyrcanus. Yet the idealized portrait of a coming priest-king, projected here and elsewhere in the twelve testaments, was apparently inspired by the successes of the early Maccabees. The portrait, moreover, reflects messianic expectations analogous to those expressed in the Parables of Enoch, except that here the messiah is actually a man and not a preexistent heavenly anthropoid. According to the hymn, the expected new priest will execute righteous judgment as a king (v. 2) whose legitimation comes directly from God (v. 6). He will shine as the sun, removing darkness, and bringing peace on earth. (V. 4.) Not only will he banish sin (v. 9), but he will bind Beliar (v. 12; cf. T. Dan 5:10), remove the sword barring Adam's return to Eden, open the gates of paradise, and give the saints access to the tree of life (T. Levi 18:10-11; cf. T. Dan 5:12). Elsewhere he is pictured as a Levite whose offices are those of priest, king, and prophet, who founds a priesthood under a new name (T. Levi 8:14-15). He will take vengeance upon the enemies of Israel (T. Dan 5:10). He will be sovereign not only over all the nation (T. Reuben 6:11), but over the Gentiles as well (T. Levi 8:14; 18:9), and his dynasty will be everlasting (Ts. Reuben 6:12; Levi 18:8).

The Testament of Judah also clearly evidences a revival of

hope that a king in the succession of Judah (ch. 24:1-6), or that the Davidic dynasty as a whole, which stems from Judah (chs. 22:2-3; 17:5-6), will be the messianic agent to bring salvation and establish the Kingdom of God. Reference to angels, demons, paradise, heaven, and hell are notably absent, however, from all passages here treating of a messiah out of Judah.

Salvation is sometimes expected in the succession of Levi and Judah jointly (Ts. Naph. 8:2-3; Sim. 7:1-3), from whom derive respectively a high-priestly and a royal dynasty (T. Judah 21:5). The idea of two messiahs as the agents of Israel's final deliverance is an extension by no means incongruous with Jewish tradition. For historical foundation of the idea, we have only to recall Zechariah's reference to " two sons of oil " (Zech. 4:14), meaning Joshua and Zerubbabel, high priest and king during the reconstruction of the Temple.

Upon the basis of present evidence, however, the origin and interrelationships of the several messianic motifs in The Testaments of the Twelve Patriarchs cannot be securely fixed, except to say that they represent a variety, possibly also a succession of public reactions to Maccabean messianic aspirations.

Noteworthy in passing is the fact that in Jewish literature the first indubitable reference to a universal resurrection of the dead occurs in the Testament of Benjamin 10:6-8. In the Testament of Dan 5:12, the term " New Jerusalem " is used for the first time.

The Psalms of Solomon. In this collection of eighteen hymns, the ideology of messianic kingship reappears, not as an interpretation of political realities, but simply as a symbol of repressed religious and political hopes for Judah's future. The messianic title occurs four times in the psalms, once in the caption of the eighteenth psalm, twice in the body of the same hymn, where prayer is made for Israel's cleansing " against the day of choice when He bringeth back His messiah " (v. 6) and praise offered for the religious and ethical renewal which will transpire in the coming generation under the rule of the Lord's messiah (vs. 8-

10). Psalm 17 specifies that the coming messiah (v. 36) will be a king in the succession of David (v. 23).

Three singularities mark the messianism of these songs. First, the psalms repudiate the messianic pretensions of the Macca-bees, who though unnamed are clearly intended. (Ps. of Sol. 17:6-14.) They are the impious impostors who have arrogantly and violently seized the throne divinely destined for the seed of David. (Vs. 6-7.) God's vengeance has delivered them and their children to a foreign enemy, who has taken them captive into the west. (Vs. 8-15.) The circumstances suggest Aristobulus II, whom Pompey took in chains to Rome, along with all his chil-dren save Alexander, who managed to escape.[36]

As a second novel feature, Ps. 17 draws a personalized por-trait of this coming Davidic messiah, in whom will be fulfilled all the hopes traditionally invested in the dynasty as a whole or in its living representative. The details of this portrait amount to an idealized version of the attributes and offices ascribed to the reigning monarch in the period of the ancient Hebrew kings.[37] The coming king will shatter the unrighteous rulers of Judah and purge Jerusalem of foreign oppressors. (Vs. 24, 26, 51.) He will bring the pagan peoples under his yoke, making Jerusalem the center of a glorious world empire. (Vs. 32-33.) He will smite the earth with the word of his mouth so that all nations will fear him. (Vs. 38-39.) He will gather the dispersed of his people (vs. 34, 50), distribute Palestine among the tribes (v. 30), expel from their midst both unrighteous Jews (v. 26) and all foreigners (v. 31), so that among the master race there will be none wicked but only " sons of their God " (vs. 30, 36). The Messiah himself will be sinless (v. 41), mighty, and wise by the Spirit of God (v. 42). His words will be more precious than re-fined gold. (V. 48.) He will lead his people faithfully and righteously so that none stumbles (v. 45) and none oppresses his fellow Jew (v. 46). He will put no trust in armies or in the resources and implements of war (v. 37), but his hope will be in the Lord, whose vassal he will be. For the Lord is the king's King (v. 38) and the ultimate sovereign over his people (v. 51).

Because his hope will be in God, none can prevail against him.
(V. 44.)

Finally, the xenophobic utopianism of these psalms offers no
political program (cf. Ps. of Sol. 12:6; 14:1; 16:11-15), but
simply discharges the hostilities latent in Pharisaic quietism. For
these Pharisaic authors, the nerve of political action and responsibility was cut by the hope of resurrection and the fear of final
judgment (Ps. of Sol. 13:9-11; 15:15; 16:1-3), though the imagery of resurrection is never integrated into their picture of the
messianic age. Their quietistic utopian dream, however, was to
become a spur to violent political action among activists of the
Zealot type.[38]

Reflections of social and political conditions, especially numerous veiled references to Pompey (Ps. of Sol. 2:30; 8:18;
12:1; 17:9, 15), are generally taken as evidence that the Psalms
of Solomon were written by Pharisees around the middle of the
first century B.C., shortly following Pompey's unnatural death in
Egypt.[39]

THE APOCALYPTIC MESSIANISM OF THE QUMRAN COMMUNITY

The scrolls found in the caves of Qumran, from 1947 onward, constitute the remains of a once larger library of Old Testament and other religious writings collected by the Essenes, it
is generally supposed, who had their headquarters at the site.
Among the non-Biblical scrolls are a number of manuscripts
that reflect the organization, discipline, theology, and history of
the community itself. Chief among these are the Community
Rule (sometimes entitled the Manual of Discipline),[40] the Damascus Rule (also known as the Zadokite Work),[41] the Messianic Rule, the War Rule, and several of the Old Testament
commentaries.

One entered the Community by joining a congregation, the
basic unit of organization. Any man born a Jew could apply for
membership. His admission depended upon his knowledge and

love of the Law and upon his submission to the rigorous rules of the order (CR vi [81–82]). Apparently at some later date proselytes were also admissible (DR xiv [116]). The applicant had first to pass screening and instruction by the Examiner (*paqid*) (CR vi [81]) or by the Overseer or Guardian (*mebaq-qer*) (DR xv [108]). The acceptable candidate voluntarily entered the Covenant by swearing " to return with all his heart and soul to every commandment of the Law of Moses in accordance with all that has been revealed of it to the sons of Zadok " (CR v [79]; DR xv [108]). Next he had to stand before the governing Council of the Congregation for examination by the session. If he passed, he was placed upon probation and again examined a year later. The successful candidate was admitted to a second year of probation, during which his property and earnings were held in escrow by the Bursar (*mebaqqer*) (CR vi [82]). If he sustained his third annual examination, he was enrolled in the Community, assigned to his appropriate rank and task, admitted to the communal table, given voice in the assembly, and his property merged with Community holdings. (*Ibid.*) Strict economic communism was compromised, whether for certain types of congregations, or at a later time for the Community as a whole, is no longer certain (DR xiii [116]).

Every member was examined yearly as to his practice of the Law and his obedience to those in ranks above his own. He was advanced or demoted accordingly. Each was required to rebuke his companion (bread-fellow) " in truth, humility, and charity." He must do so on the very day of the offense or else share the guilt. None might accuse another before the Congregation unless he had first admonished him in the presence of witnesses (CR v, vi [80]). Periodic Community Inquests were guided by detailed codes, specifying rules of conduct, and, for their breach, penalties ranging from simple penance or temporary exclusion from the communal meal to excommunication or even death (CR vi, vii [82–85]; cf. DR xv, xvi, ix–xiv [108–117]).

There is no reference to women or to marriage in the Community Rule. Celibacy might be inferred. The Damascus Rule speaks of some members, at least, who lived in camps " according to the rule of the Land," marrying, and having children (DR vi [103]); but no man was allowed to marry a second woman while his first wife was still alive (DR iv [101]).

Ultimate authority in matters of doctrine, property, and discipline was curiously balanced between a Zadokite priestly aristocracy and the membership at large (CR v [78–79]). Not all " sons of Zadok " joined the sect (Midrash on the Last Days i [247]). Those who did join constituted, nominally at least, the governing elite of the communal hierarchy: " The sons of Aaron alone shall command in matters of justice and property, and every rule concerning the men of the Community shall be determined according to their word " (CR ix [87]). They were the recipients and interpreters of special revelations as to the meaning of the Law of Moses (CR v [79]); they served both as preceptors and exemplars of the way of righteousness (Liturgical Fragments iii [207]), and as interpreters of the esoteric teachings of the sect, supposing that the Master or instructor (*maskil*) was also a priest (CR ix [88]).

Details of organizational structure and function are not always clear. Not only does the Qumran mother colony seem to have been represented by satellite groups in the cities and towns of Judah, leading probably to local differentiations, but the basic documents of the sect cover an extended period during which the structures and aims of the whole sect may well have varied. A quorum of ten members was required for any meeting of the local congregation (CR vi [81]), called also a " camp " in the Damascus Rule (DR xiii [115]). Each congregation regularly assembled daily to spend one third of every night in communal reading of the Book, study of the Law, and prayer. They were seated according to rank, in which the priests came first. No session could proceed in the absence (1) of a priest, and (2) of a man thoroughly competent in the interpretation and application of the Law (CR vi [81]). It appears that, ideally, each congregation was ruled by a priest (*hakohen*) who was also versed in the Law (DR xiii [115]), who not only presided over its sessions

and at the communal meal of bread and wine, but acted also as
the Overseer (*mebaqqer*) in all matters of communal discipline (CR vi [81]). Yet, practically, a congregation might have
no priest qualified to interpret and administer the Law in such a
communal setting. In that case a qualified Levite might be appointed as Guardian or Overseer (*mebaqqer*) to rule over the
camp (DR xiii [115]). There seems to have been an Overseer
(*mebaqqer*) over all the camps (DR xiv [116]); and there are
suggestions of a general assembly comprising the elite of the entire sect (MR i, ii [120]). There is debate, however, as to the
functions and interrelationships of the *hakohen, mebaqqer, paqid, maskil* — if, indeed, the latter title applies to an office at
all.[42] The idealized picture of the Community as it will appear in
the messianic age (MR i [120]) sheds little light on its actual
organizational structure.

The sect was apparently too engrossed in speculation about
the " coming " messianic age to bother with chronicling their
own. Allusions to persons and events touching the life of the
Community are casually woven into their messianic theology.
For brevity of treatment, we leave them intertwined. A few of
the references are specific, as, for example, those to the " chief
of the kings of Greece " (DR viii [105]), to Demetrius and to
Antiochus (Comm. on Nahum i [231–232]). But many of the
allusions are deliberately obscure, after the manner of The
Book of Daniel, and for similar reasons.

The dualism of Essene theology, suggesting connections with
Zoroastrianism, is especially marked in the Community Rule
(CR iii, iv [75–78]). Here God is pictured as predetermining all
things whatsoever — their existence, design, time, and task.
(The same determinism of future events by divine plan is affirmed in the Damascus Rule ii [98].) Though he created man
to govern the world, he made his heart the battleground between
the two spirits of good and evil. God himself made the two spirits, the one of light and truth, the other of darkness and falsehood. To every man he apportioned some of each spirit, and
every man's destiny depends upon the proportion of his inheri-

tance in each realm. That proportion, again, is a function of a man's origin, for there are two kinds of men. The " children of righteousness," born of truth and sprung from a fountain of light, are ruled by the Prince of Light, and walk in the ways of light. The " children of falsehood," born of falsehood and sprung from a source of darkness, are ruled by the Angel of Darkness and walk in his ways (CR iii [75–76]), toward which they have a native inclination (*yetzer*) (WR xiii [141]).

This dualism is seen to issue in " two ways " of life, one of rigoristic Jewish piety, the other of blasphemous impiety (CR iv [76–77]). The life style of the " sons of light," instinct with a fear of the Law of God, exhibits a spirit of humility, patience, trust in all the deeds of God, zeal for righteousness, stringent purity, abundant charity toward the " sons of truth." An " everlasting hatred in a spirit of secrecy for the men of perdition " is a mark of status (CR ix [88]), for the " saints " characteristically hate all " sons of darkness " (CR i [72]). The wicked way of life manifests a spirit of greed, lies, deceit, arrogance, cruelty, ill-temper, brazen insolence, lust, lewdness, dullness of ear, blindness of eye, and a blasphemous tongue.

The alternations of day and night, and of the lunar and solar seasons, are interpreted as physical signs of the light-darkness dualism (CR x [89]).

The strife between light and darkness produces a split in time itself. Now is the time of Satan's dominion (CR i, ii [72, 74]), and of God's wrath. In accordance with the mysterious will of God, the Angel of Darkness exercises, until his end, some control even over the righteous; he leads all of them astray, causes all their sins and unlawful deeds, as well as their distresses, afflictions, persecutions (CR iii [76]). But God has foreordained an end for falsehood; at the " time of his visitation," he will destroy it forever. Then those who walk in darkness will be turned over to the destroying angels, and consigned to everlasting damnation, eternal torment, and the fire of the dark regions. After the appointed time of judgment, truth will reign supreme forever. God himself will root out falsehood from the flesh of the righteous, cleanse them of their wicked deeds, crown them with glory, clothe them with majesty, endow them with everlasting life in light unending (CR iv [76–78]; cf. WR i [124–125]).

In the meantime, men of the Community of God, i.e., the sons of light (CR i [72]; cf. DR i, iv, vi [97, 100, 103]), have withdrawn from the world of ungodly men " into the wilderness to prepare the way of Him; as it is written: *Prepare in the wilderness the way of . . . make straight in the desert a path for our God* (Isa. 50:3) " (CR viii [86]). This path is understood to mean " the study of the Law which He commanded by the hand of Moses," knowledge of which alone enables a man to live in accord with all that God has revealed from age to age.

The original nucleus of this wilderness sect seems to have been a group of Zadokite priests, joined by a number of Levites, who withdrew from Judah (DR iv [100]) in protest against the lax piety of the ruling party in Jerusalem. Yet for the first twenty years, by their own account, they themselves were " like blind men groping for the way," until there arose among them the Teacher of Righteousness (DR i [97–98]). This proto-Essene group was numbered, possibly, among the Hasidim mentioned in I Macc. 2:42; 7:13-14, in connection with the Antiochian persecutions.

The distinctive Essene ideology was apparently formulated by this Teacher of Righteousness, a priest, who convinced his fellows that they were living in the last days before the final Messianic Kingdom and that everything then happening had been secretly foretold in the ancient Hebrew Scriptures (Comm. on Hab. i [236]). To him alone God had made known " all the mysteries of the words of His servants the Prophets " (Comm. on Hab. vii [239]). His characteristic exegetical method, passed on to his followers, was the " explanation " (*peser*), communicating a privately revealed meaning supposedly hidden even from the author of the Scriptural passage under consideration.[48] The system of " truths " derived in this way was carefully concealed even from fellow Jews, excepting those who entered the

Covenant and submitted to the rule of the order (CR iv, ix [76, 88]).

The Essene schismatics understood themselves to be under a Covenant of Grace (CR i [72]), members, therefore, of a New Covenant (DR vi, viii [103, 107]), the true remnant of Israel (WR xiii [141]; DR i, ii [97–98]). They also identified themselves as the Poor (WR xi [138]; Comm. on Hab. xii [242]; Comm. on Ps. 37 [244]). Fellow Jews who accepted neither the doctrine of the Teacher of Righteousness nor his interpretation of the Mosaic law, they identified as the " congregation of traitors, . . . who departed from the way " (DR i [97]). These nonbelievers they lumped with the wicked, and consigned them to utter destruction; after all, God himself hated them and led them astray. Believers alone were destined to survive (DR ii [98]). Adherents of the Teacher were expected to prevail over all other people (DR viii [107–108]). The blessed Poor (i.e., the Essenes) would inherit the earth (Comm. on Ps. 37 [244]). Fanatic adherence to the teachings of their founder is again apparent in a comment on Hab. 2:4b: " But the righteous shall live by his faith." The Essene explanation (*peser*) identifies the righteous as " those who observe the Law in the House of Judah," whom God will deliver in the Last Day " because of their suffering and because of their faith in the Teacher of Righteousness " (Comm. on Hab. viii [239]).

The sect cherished a bitter animus against a Jerusalem official called the Spouter, a cryptic title deviously derived from Micah 2:6. This individual not only approved the amassing of wealth, but sanctioned and probably himself practiced divorce and remarriage — both heinous offenses in the eyes of the Essenes (DR iv, v [101]). This Spouter of Lies outraged the " elect of God " by leading the simple astray in these matters of the Law (Comm. on Hab. x [241]; Comm. on Micah [231]); this Scoffer spread over Israel a flood of lies (DR i [97]). A partisan group, the House of Absolom, was castigated because they were silent when the Teacher was brought to trial and punishment by the

MESSIANIC THEOLOGY AND CHRISTIAN FAITH

Liar (Comm. on Hab. v [238]), who earlier had come into con-
flict with the Teacher over questions of law and doctrine (*ibid.,*
ii [236]). The Wicked Priest was apparently another name for
the same ruler. This Wicked Priest seemed at first to share the
sect's point of view; but once in office, he committed offenses
analogous to those named above (*ibid.,* viii [240]). In the consequent partisan strife, the Wicked Priest pursued the Teacher of
Righteousness into exile and sought to embarrass him before
his congregation on the Sabbath preceding the Day of Atone-
ment (Comm. on Hab. xi [241–242]).[44] He even tried unsuc-
cessfully to have the Teacher put to death (Comm. on Ps. 37
[245]), but was himself eventually delivered to his enemies,
among whom he suffered a horrible death, " because of the iniquity committed against the Teacher of Righteousness and the
men of his Council " (Comm. on Hab. ix [240]).

The Teacher of Righteousness is apparently once alluded to
as messiah: " By the hand of thy *mashiah,* who discerned Thy
testimonies, Thou hast revealed to us the [times] of the battle of
Thy hands that Thou mayest glorify Thyself in our enemies by
levelling the hordes of Satan, the seven nations of vanity, by the
hand of Thy poor whom Thou hast redeemed " (WR xi [138]).
Whether or not it applies to him, the allusion is only to a priestly
anointing and does not identify a coming eschatological Messiah. There are other references to " anointed ones " whose functions are priestly or prophetic, but not eschatological (DR ii
[98]; vi [102]).

Yet there is also speculation as to the role of the Messiah in
Israel's eschatological existence. In this speculation, the emphasis falls variously upon the three cultic offices of priest, king, and
prophet, induction into each of which was traditionally by the
rite of anointing.

In the Messianic Rule, a visionary manual of protocol for the
coming age, the high priest is referred to (MR ii [121]) [45] simply as the Anointed (i.e., the [priestly] Messiah). At any assembly of the Council in the eschatological period he is to take
precedence over the king, referred to as the Messiah of Israel,[46]

entering before him and sitting in the seat of highest honor. When he is present at any banquet of state, or at any meal where at least ten men are gathered, he is to bless and extend his hand over the bread and wine before all others, even the king (*ibid.*).

According to the Community Rule, the dawn of the coming age will coincide with the advent of three persons, clearly identified as the Prophet and *two* messiahs, the one priestly, stemming from Aaron, the other royal and political, stemming from Israel. The doctrine and discipline of the Community are oriented toward their coming. Thus the men of holiness, who walk in the way of perfection, " shall be ruled by the primitive precepts in which the men of the Community were first instructed until there shall come the Prophet and the Messiahs (*mashihe*) of Aaron and Israel " (CR ix [87]).[47] The Prophet would seem to be simply the precursor and legitimator of the coming Messiah, a conception reflecting the Elijah *redivivus* of Mal. 4:5 and the announcement by Moses of the coming of a prophet like himself (Deut. 18:18-19); [48] for elsewhere the promulgation of God's will in the eschatological age is clearly the function, not of the Prophet, but of the priestly Messiah, who as the Interpreter of the Law is to rule conjointly with the Branch of David at the end of time (Midrash on the Last Days i [246]).[49]

The anticipation of two Messiahs is reflected also in the Liturgical Fragments attached originally to the Scroll of the Community Rule. In a proleptic blessing of the coming royal Messiah, here called the Prince (*nasi*) of the congregation after the usage in Ezekiel,[50] the whole ideology of ancient Hebrew kingship is picked up and projected as the expected shape of the political sphere in the coming age (Liturgical Fragments v [209]).[51] A parallel blessing of the high priest suggests both his current and his eschatological role (*ibid.,* iii [207]).

The Damascus Rule makes evident, on the other hand, that at some time in the history of the sect some scribe thought it proper to attribute to a single individual both the royal and the priestly eschatological roles. Reference is made to the statutes in which the Community is to walk " [. . . *until the coming of the Mes-*

sia]h of Aaron and Israel who will pardon their iniquity " (DR xiv [117]), and the singular (*mashiah*) found here is confirmed by a fragment discovered at Qumran.[52]

Though there is no conclusive evidence that the schismatics ever identified the Teacher of Righteousness with the coming Messiah, the former nevertheless played a significant role in their eschatological speculation. They regarded themselves as living already in the troublous period preceding the end of the present age: " At the end of forty years [the wicked] shall be blotted out and not an [evil] man shall be found on earth " (Comm. on Ps. 37 [243]). They tended to date the beginning of their time of trouble at the death of their Teacher, and its end, of course, at the coming of the Messiah of Aaron and Israel (DR (B) i, ii [106]). They envisioned their return to Jerusalem as precipitating a war in which all Jews who defected to the Liar would be destroyed. Hence, on the analogy of Israel's " forty years " in the desert after the exodus from Egypt (Deut. 2:14) and the consequent conquest of Palestine, the exiles expected to end their stay in the wilderness and retake Jerusalem about forty years after the Teacher's death (DR vi [107]). When the time lapsed and their expectations proved false, they evidently turned to the prophets to show by devious exegesis that the delay had been cryptically forecast all along (Comm. on Hab. vii [239]).

Whether or not the Essenes were actively involved in Zealotic uprisings in the first centuries B.C. and A.D.,[53] their late writings tended to be politically inflammatory. The War Rule, for example, is a xenophobic revenge fantasy in the guise of a manual for the conduct of the coming messianic war. When the great attack is unleashed, the " exiled sons of light " will return from the Desert of the Gentiles (Qumran) to encamp in the Desert of Jerusalem against the Kittim and their allies, the ruling party in Jerusalem, all of whom will be vanquished without survivor (WR i [124]; cf. xviii [146–147]).[54] " At that time, the assembly of gods and the hosts of men shall battle, causing great carnage; on the day of calamity, the sons of light shall battle with the company of darkness amid the shouts of a mighty multitude and the clamour of gods and men to (make manifest) the might of God " (WR i [125]). The gods would seem to mean angels, for it is said that God himself will muster Israel militant (the Essenes), together with the saints and angels in heaven (WR xii [139]), against Satan and his evil hosts (WR iii, xviii [141, 146]).

The action will escalate into forty years of war against all nations of earth (WR i, ii [125–126]); cf. xv, xvi [143–144]). The Prince of the congregation, i.e., the royal Messiah, will bear the martial standard (WR v [130]) as the Hero of war whose sword devours the flesh of sinners and fills his palaces with precious booty (WR xii [139–140]). The high priest, i.e., the priestly Messiah, will pronounce the " Prayer in Time of War " as a pontifical blessing, and his fellow Zadokites will serve as morale officers (WR xv [143–144]), sounding " the trumpets of Massacre " among the fighting men (WR xvi [145]).

This " battle of God " (WR ix [135]) is viewed as a predestined miracle (WR xviii [147]), the outcome of which will be " eternal deliverance for the company of God, but destruction for all the nations of wickedness " (WR xv [143]). Though the saints are to do the fighting, their power in battle will come from God. " Truly, the battle is Thine! Their bodies are crushed by the might of Thy hand and there is no man to bury them " (WR xi [137–138]). The revenge fantasy encompasses either genocide for all peoples not counted among the redeemed remnant, a destruction of all sons of darkness (WR xiii [141]), or the survival of a remnant of the Gentiles (WR xi [139]) privileged to be under the benign yoke of the Lord and of Israel forever (WR xii [140]). History finds its consummation in the everlasting dominion of God himself, the King of Glory, over the faithful of his Covenant (WR xii [139]). " His exalted greatness shall shine eternally to the peace, blessing, glory, joy, and long life of all the sons of light." (WR i [124].)

The Essene sectarian writings are generally thought to have originated between 175 B.C., or shortly before that, down to about 40 B.C.[55] Vermes, following R. de Vaux, reports archaeological data indicating: (1) that the Qumran settlement was founded between 150–100 B.C., upon the deserted ruins of a town belonging to the ancient kings of Judah; (2) that community life was disrupted by an earthquake; (3) that the buildings were restored and enlarged during the reign of Archelaus (4 B.C. to A.D. 6), and fully occupied until burned, probably by the Romans, in A.D. 68 during the first Jewish revolt (A.D. 66–70); (4) that thereafter for a few years Roman soldiers were quartered in the ruins; (5) that the last semipermanent residents were the followers of Bar-Cochba, who took refuge there during the second Jewish revolt (A.D. 132–135).[56] The scrolls discovered in the caves are scribal copies, buried not later than A.D. 68, when the Essenes abandoned the site.

Essene messianic ideology, and the community organization based upon it, was too inflexible to survive the destruction of the Jerusalem Temple in A.D. 70.

Numerous dates and identifications have been proposed for the principal persons and events alluded to in these sectarian writings, especially the Teacher of Righteousness.[57] There possibly will never be agreement as to his identity, and estimates as to the time of his ministry range from 175 B.C., when Antiochus Epiphanes mounted the Seleucid throne, to 63 B.C., when Pompey entered Jerusalem.[58] There is corresponding disagreement as to what enemy is cryptically designated the Kittim — whether the Seleucids or the Romans, though the latter seem more probable.[59]

In any case, it is clearly evident that Qumran theology was firmly embedded in the milieu out of which New Testament messianism arose. Elements of New Testament thought earlier attributed to Gentile Gnostic influence are now seen to have been long current in Jerusalem. That John the Baptist was an Essene is by no means inconceivable. The light-darkness, truth-falsehood motifs in the Johannine literature evidence familiarity with Qumran theology, as do many details in the eschatology of the book of Revelation. The letters of Paul suggest a knowledge of Essene dualistic anthropology and angelology. The Letter to the Hebrews could well have been written by an Essene convert to Christianity. We next turn to consider, then, what transformations in messianic theology were wrought around the person and teachings of Jesus.

Chapter V

New Testament Messianism

Methodologically critical studies of the New Testament have produced a few significant findings upon which there is a fairly general scholarly consensus. Current discussions of New Testament messianism take for granted some familiarity with those findings, and some knowledge of the presuppositions which guide further research.

It is generally acknowledged, for example, that the New Testament writings should be classed, not as history, but as preaching (*kērygma*). This preaching was produced over an extended period of time in response to a variety of concrete circumstances. Consequently, its content is not homogeneous but stratified. Since New Testament kerygma, however, is basically a product of religious imagination responding in particular circumstances, it not only preserves traces of transformations in preaching content, but incorporates as well many historically authentic memories of contemporary persons and events. In an attempt to reconstruct the history of primitive Christian messianism, therefore, the first problem is to distinguish the several strata of preaching, and then to examine specific messianic ideas in relation to the particular life situations (*Sitze im Leben*) out of which they arose.

Research has made it evident that historical reconstruction must begin with the Synoptic Gospels, not with the Gospel of John. Even the Synoptics were written comparatively late; certain of Paul's letters, for example, antedate them. Their historical value lies in the fact that they incorporate blocks of material lifted out of the earliest strata of Christian preaching. In the lowest stratum, we have authentic sayings of Jesus, his own preaching. At the next level, we find examples of Palestinian kerygma in which Jesus the Preacher is himself preached for the first time, with the consequence that memories of Jesus' words and deeds tend to be transformed in the light of the community's new understanding of him. At the third level, we find Hellenistic kerygma which translates Aramaic Jewish conceptions of Jesus into the Greek language and Gentile thought forms. At the fourth level, we have the creative reinterpretation of all earlier preaching by the Synoptist himself, who freely employs the several traditions to communicate his own message.

Certain literary-critical presuppositions guide continuing efforts to distinguish the several strata of preaching within the Synoptics. It is still taken for granted: (1) that Mark is the oldest of the Gospels; (2) that Matthew and Luke each reproduces sections from Mark; (3) that they make common use of still another source (*Quelle,* " Q " for short), which probably existed as somewhat variant collections of the sayings of Jesus; and (4) that Q, although unused by Mark, is older than his Gospel. Finally, Q is now seen to contain the preaching of Jesus as well as his ethical teaching (*didachē*).[1]

It is further assumed that the authentic preaching of Jesus can be distinguished from later kerygmatic reformulations by the application of three tests.[2] Anything in the sayings of Jesus which presupposes the post-Easter situation, or which reflects the post-Easter faith of the church, is eliminated as historically unauthentic. Likewise eliminated is anything in his sayings for which parallels can be found in contemporary Judaism. Finally, any saying that passes the first two tests should exhibit Aramaic linguistic features; the presumption of authenticity is increased if the saying reflects the structure of Aramaic poetry.

The use of the principal messianic titles in the Synoptic Gospels has been subjected to these tests, with results which have been succinctly summarized by Hans Conzelmann.[3]

The first question at issue is twofold: 1. Have we any evidence that Jesus used the titles at all, and if so, does the evidence indicate whether he referred the titles to himself or to another? 2. Is there evidence that, prior to Easter, the disciples themselves applied any of the titles to Jesus?

Christos, first of the four titles dealt with, does not appear in Q at all. Critical examination discloses, as Conzelmann further summarizes the findings, that most occurrences elsewhere in the Synoptics can be dismissed without further ado as the work of later redactors in the post-Easter situation (comparing, e.g., Matt. 16:20 with Mark 8:30). Mark 9:41; 13:21; 15:32 and such parallels as may be found in Matthew and Luke are likewise dismissed as secondary.

In three cases only does Conzelmann find reason to debate the possibility that the term was used in the pre-Easter situation. The first instance is Peter's confession that Jesus is the Christ (Mark 8:27 ff. and parallels). In all the Synoptics, however, this narrative depends upon the creative interpretation of the traditions by Mark himself and has, therefore, no value as historical evidence that the title was actually applied prior to Easter. The incident is a dramatic statement of the post-Easter faith of the community, lacking any concrete historical detail. In the second debatable instance (Mark 12:35-37 and parallels), the dramatic action turns upon a fanciful understanding that Ps. 110:1 is David's prediction of the coming Messiah. Jesus is represented as asking how the Christ can be David's son when David himself calls him Lord. The structure of the question betrays its catechetical purpose and implies an answer such as appears in the Christological formula cited by Paul in Rom. 1:3 ff. The incident is another fanciful invention expressing the post-Easter faith. The third debatable instance has its setting in the examination of Jesus by the Sanhedrin, where the high priest asks: " Are you the Christ? " (Mark 14:61 and parallels). Conzelmann's analysis, following Bultmann and Dibelius, leads to the conclusion that the Synoptic accounts of Passion Week evidence the reinterpretation of the events in the light of the post-Easter faith of the disciples. The high priest's question and Jesus' answer alike belong to an imaginative reconstruction of the Sanhedrin scene.

The Son of Man is the second messianic title with which Conzelmann deals. He notes the occurrence of this concept in all strata of Synoptic preaching: both in Mark and Q, and in the kerygmatic traditions peculiar to Matthew and Luke. He discovers, however, no critical apparatus by which we can be sure in specific uses whether the Synoptists found the term in the sources they employ, or whether they themselves inserted the concept as a part of their own creative reconstructions of the sources. In many instances the latter is clearly the case. It is significant, however, that the concept is virtually never used in the New Testament, except in the four Gospels; and there it occurs only in words attributed to Jesus. This would seem to constitute presumptive evidence that the title stood, in some instances at least, not only in the primitive kerygma of the disciples, but also in the authentic sayings of Jesus. The question arises, then, as to the various ways in which the title is used.[4]

Conzelmann notes that the transmitted " Son of Man " sayings divide themselves into three groups. The first group deals with the contemporary activity of the Son of Man on earth. (Mark 2:10, 28, etc., and parallels; Q: Matt. 8:20 and parallel in Luke 9:58.) These reflect post-Easter thinking, for in numerous instances the technical meaning is demonstrably superimposed upon sayings which in the original Aramaic expression meant simply man in general. (Cf. Mark 2:28; Matt. 8:20.) The second group deals with Jesus' coming passion. (Lacking in Q; found in Mark 8:31; 9:31; 10:33; 9:9; etc., and parallels.) One cannot defend the authenticity of these sayings simply on the grounds that Jesus must have foreseen his coming rendezvous with death. For these sayings do not constitute a sharp analysis of actual circumstances, but proclaim rather a divine preordination of the passion of Jesus. They are to be seen, therefore, not as predictions before the fact, but as kerygmatic " prophecies " arising out of the event itself — *vaticinia ex eventu*. They superimpose upon the passion narratives an understanding achieved only after Easter. The third group speaks of the coming (parousia) of the Son of Man upon the clouds of heaven (Mark 8:38; 13:26; 14:62, and parallels; Q: Matt. 24:27, 36, and parallel in Luke 17:24, 26; special sources: Matt. 10:23; Luke 17:22). Conzelmann holds, in effect, that the idea of the Son of Man's coming on the clouds of heaven derives obviously from Dan. 7:13; and that all uses of the concept in reference to Jesus are unintelligible apart from a post-Easter reinterpretation in which the exaltation of Jesus to heaven is presupposed. He notes that Jesus himself always speaks of the *coming* Son of Man as *another than himself*. In view of the fact that the community later awaited the return of Jesus as the coming Son of Man, he concludes with Bultmann that the sayings which distinguish the two are the authentic words of Jesus. It is noteworthy that Synoptic apocalypticism, unlike the Jewish, limits the heavenly existence of the Son of Man to the period between ascension and the final Parousia.

Once it is determined that post-Easter theology underlies all Synoptic identifications of Jesus as the Son of Man, in the technical meaning of the term, we have still to consider the fact that the title never appears except in words attributed to Jesus. No one uses the term as a title by which to address him. Conzelmann concludes, in summary, that the title functions to express the community's post-Easter belief that Jesus is shortly to return as the Son of Man on the clouds of heaven. Unlike the terms "Christ" and "Son of God," this concept does not function explicitly as a confessional title, to acknowledge what Jesus already is in the community's faith. It serves rather to announce the community's expectation of what he will soon prove himself to be, since obviously he has never yet appeared on the clouds.

The "Servant of God" title derives, of course, from the Servant Songs in Second Isaiah. It has long been supposed that Jesus understood his own ministry, and especially his coming suffering, in the light of what is there said about the sufferings of the Servant of Yahweh. Conzelmann notes, however, that this

title is completely missing in the older strata of Synoptic kerygma. Where it is once directly employed in the latest stratum,
it serves to characterize Jesus, not as the Suffering Servant, but
as the Savior. (Matt. 12:18 ff.) Though the late stratum of Synoptic tradition deals occasionally, if only sparingly, with Isa.,
ch. 53, it never treats of the " Servant of God " title as such.
Isaiah 53:4 is actually quoted in Matt. 8:17, without express
allusion to the Servant of God and with no reference whatever to
the passion of Jesus. There is no support in the sources for the
hypothesis that Jesus actually thought of himself as the Servant
of God in the meaning of Second Isaiah.

The title " Son of God," Conzelmann points out, was not
among the current Jewish designations for the coming Messiah
in the time of Jesus. All accounts by the Synoptists of the use of
the title in reference to Jesus stand under the suspicion of being
post-Easter formulations of the Christian community. That holds
true for the utterance of the title by the demons (Mark 3:11, etc.,
and parallels), for its use in the parable of the vineyard (Mark
12:6 and parallels [following Kümmel]), in the trial (Mark
14:61 and parallels),[5] and in the accounts of the several epipha-
nies associated with the baptism, temptation, and transfiguration
of Jesus. As used in the last group, the concept implies adoption: by means of a *present* declaration from heaven, Jesus *becomes* the Son of God. (In this respect the usage conforms to the
ideology of ancient Hebrew kingship, which it reflects.) The idea
of a preexistent Son of God who comes down from heaven to
earth is here completely absent. The usage in Matt. 11:25-27
and parallel in Luke 10:21 f. is exceptional. Here, indeed, Sonship implies preexistence, but it also clearly implies the Hellenistic notion of a mutual relationship of " knowing " between Father and Son. Inferentially, the passage exhibits a comparatively
late translation of Palestinian preaching into Hellenistic thought
forms.

The question of Sonship, Conzelmann concedes, must also be
posed in a wider context. Does the manner in which Jesus speaks
of God as his Father imply a consciousness that he is in a unique

sense the Son of God? That he characterized God as Father is, in itself, nothing strange in Jewish thought. Did he, however, speak of " his " Father in an exclusive sense? According to the Synoptists, he did. He spoke on the one hand of " my " Father (Matt. 7:21), and on the other of " your " Father (Matt. 5:45); but he never linked himself together with his audience — " our " Father. This usage proves to be, however, a stylistic distinction superimposed by the post-Easter community; most of the passages where the Father title appears are secondary. Attention is next directed to Jesus' use of " Abba," a familiar form of address implying an intimacy with God otherwise unprecedented in Judaism — as if we were to call God " Papa." This usage, however, was not exclusively his (following H. Braun); the community also used " Abba " as a form of address (Rom. 8:15). Although Jesus doubtless possessed the consciousness of a singular relationship with God, this evidently came to expression only indirectly.

THE MESSIANIC SECRET IN MARK

According to Mark, Jesus knew that he was the Messiah and the Son of God, but never openly identified himself as such until at his trial, when he was asked by the high priest, " Are you the Christ, the Son of the Blessed? " he answered, " I am " (Mark 14:61-62 and parallels). Mark was prepared, therefore, to see in Jesus' use of the " Son of Man " title a cryptic disclosure of his secret identity. This notion of a " messianic secret " which only slowly came to light crops up in Mark's account of the healing miracles (ch. 7:36) and in his report that Jesus restrained the demons from revealing his identity (ch. 3:11-12 and parallels). Conzelmann points out that the notion itself is full of contradictions and inconceivable as a historical fact. More to the point, it does not appear in the older traditions, but only in Mark's explanatory narrative. Though the idea is Mark's invention, its purpose was not, as Wrede thought, to bring his unmessianic source material into conformity with his own messianic views.

His Palestinian sources already had explicit messianic content. The invention intended, rather, to reveal the meaning of the fact that the messianism in the preaching of Jesus differs from that of the post-Easter kerygma.[6] Mark's theory of the " messianic secret," in fact, gave him the most trouble just at those points where the earlier tradition was most definitely messianic, as in the account of the transfiguration, for example (ch. 9:9-13).

Publication of Conzelmann's article, of course, did not bring to an end all further historicocritical research upon the use of the various messianic titles in the several strata of Synoptic tradition. Debate continues, moreover, not only as to specific details, but as to the historical implications of the findings established by such research as well. Yet it remains abundantly clear that the express use of messianic titles, as such, by others in reference to Jesus, and by Jesus in reference to himself, are anachronistic constructions superimposed upon the sources by the post-Easter Christian community.[7]

JESUS AS AN APOCALYPTIC PREACHER

The results of such research are by no means entirely negative. The hope of reconstructing a detailed life of Jesus on the basis of critical studies, it is true, has long since been abandoned. Yet his verifiably authentic preaching is now better known than at any time since the apostolic period,[8] and more evidence as to his actual behavior has been recovered than was deemed possible a few decades ago.[9] Recent surveys of findings arising from the current new quest for the historical Jesus [10] suggest a number of general conclusions regarding his preaching and his career.

When once the overlay of post-Easter reinterpretation has been removed from his authentic parables [11] and sayings (logia), it is clear not only that Jesus preached the imminent consummation of the reign of God on earth but that he declared his preaching itself to be a proleptic manifestation of the Kingdom's dawning. At times he sounded like an Essene demanding rigorous interpretation and fulfillment of Torah, specifically in the question of divorce and remarriage (Matt. 5:31-32 and parallels). The similarities are deceptive. His statement on the question is fundamentally concerned, not for the strict preservation of traditional law for its own sake, but rather for the acceptance of marriage as a covenant between partners equal as persons before God. His demand that the sons of God love their enemies because that was what God was doing (vs. 43-48 and parallels) clearly challenged the partisan and xenophobic among his hearers to a new kind of personal existence, quite different from the Essene way of life.

Still more challenging to the assumptions then underlying all current Jewish theological self-understanding was his implicit location of divine authority (*exousia*), not in tradition, but in his own creativity: " You have heard that it was said. . . . But I say." Unlike the Essenes and the Zealots, he did not preach an impending messianic war as the phenomenon ending the present age of wrath and ushering in the Kingdom. Instead of war, he viewed his own appearance as the event mediating the shift of the two ages (Matt. 11:11-13 and parallel in Luke 16:16) and providing incipient participation in the coming Kingdom.[12] He construed not only his preaching but also his personal conduct, in eating with publicans and sinners, for example, as evidencing here and now the trenchant diagnostic and therapeutic activity of God. He both preached (Matt. 5:11-12 and parallel in Luke 6:22-23) and practiced the endurance of persecution as the inevitable shape of man's service to God amid the alienations and monstrous deformities of human existence in this evil age now passing away. His understanding of divine providence (as in Matt. 6:25-34) was not, therefore, a cosmological model constructed for peace of mind, but a demand for present faith in God. Faith itself he conceived not only in terms of man's grasping, but in terms as well of an energy and meaning that grasps man and incipiently discloses itself in transforming the man thus grasped. The evidence suggests that he saw the power of this transformation, not as an exclusive and private possession, but

as latently at work in every man. It was his vocation to precipitate the crisis of decision in which alone that transforming energy comes to manifestation.

His purpose in going up to Jerusalem, therefore, was not to
fulfill some preconceived plan of salvation by committing sui-
cide. He went, rather, to pronounce diagnostic judgment upon a
sickness at the core of his own ethnoreligious establishment, and
to announce a favorable prognosis, provided his people opened
themselves up to the therapeutic energy that he dared to believe
was already at work in his own preaching and way of life. Since
he could well have known of John the Baptist's fate, he seems to
have made his challenge in Jerusalem at the calculated risk of
his life. Yet the evidence suggests that, far from courting martyrdom, he deplored the tragedy of his own death when finally
he saw it coming (Luke 13:31-33).[18]

Clearly, he did not regard himself as another like John the
Baptist, heralding an event as yet only about to happen. He
preached judgment and salvation as an occurrence already beginning in himself. This his disciples later remembered and believed. Yet just as clearly he also preached the imminent coming of the Son of Man, another than himself, who would immediately bring an end to the present evil age, now already passing
away, and quickly consummate the salvation now already occurring in his own life and work. Moreover, if we grant the case
for the authenticity of Mark 14:25 and parallels in Matt. 26:29;
Luke 22:16, 18,[14] he believed on the eve of his now certain crucifixion that he would soon rise from the dead to join his disciples at wine in the Kingdom of God — established presumably
by the early advent of the expected Son of Man. In these beliefs
he was clearly mistaken, if in nothing else than the shortness of
time. The evil age may still be passing, but it has not yet passed
away. The Son of Man has not yet come upon the clouds of
heaven. The dawning Kingdom has not yet been consummated.

THE PREACHER HIMSELF AS THE CHRIST

Jesus announced, and his early disciples believed, that his preaching and his way of life were in themselves manifestations of the diagnostic and curative activity of God. His crucifixion, however, raised the question of the sovereignty of God in a radically different way. Was his dying a completely unhygienic episode, a tragic and senseless defeat of the healing energy operative in human existence, presumptive evidence that there is in fact no such energy? Or was his death itself ultimately a diacritic and therapeutic event? Was the meaning of this particular man's crucifixion an occasion for despair or for hope in God? The understanding of the New Testament answer to these questions turns upon what is meant by the disciples' belief in the resurrection and exaltation of Jesus.

His resurrection is never directly mentioned in the Q material. Indirect allusion to it occurs in Mark 14:25 and cognate expressions in Matthew and Luke, where in the face of death he declares: " I shall not drink again of the fruit of the vine until that day when I drink it new in the kingdom of God." Though probably authentic, nothing in the saying implies that he understood his resurrection in terms other than those of the general resurrection expected at the coming of the Son of Man with whom he did not identify himself. The evidence indicates that he became the Christ and was first provisionally identified as the Son of Man in the post-Easter faith of the community. Moreover, his death was not understood as itself a salvation event, either in Q or in the earliest Palestinian preaching of him as the Christ, as the latter is evidenced in the sermons recorded in the opening chapters of The Acts. His suffering and death were not at first understood in terms of Isa., ch. 53, but rather in terms of the " stone " saying in Ps. 118:22-23: " The stone which the builders rejected has become the head of the corner. This is the Lord's doing; it is marvelous in our eyes " (cf. Mark 12:10-11; Acts 4:11).[15] Yet clearly the resurrection of Jesus, whatever is meant by that, underlies both the preservation of the Q material

and the earliest proclamation that the man rejected and crucified was in fact the promised Messiah.

An examination of the accounts of the resurrection raises
questions as to the character of that event. In authentic Mark,
oldest of the Synoptics, we find no claim that Jesus ever appeared to his disciples after the crucifixion. There is evidence,
to be sure, in Mark 8:31 (and parallels) of a tradition holding
that three days after his crucifixion Jesus *would* rise again. But
this tradition itself is a postcrucifixion creation, for it now takes
for granted what was evidently never supposed before Jesus
died, namely, that he himself was the coming Son of Man. The
only events which Mark adduces as evidence that the resurrection had in fact taken place was the discovery of the empty
tomb and the report by the women of what an angel there said
to them three days after the crucifixion. Parenthetically, Paul,
writing just a few years after the crucifixion, preserves a confessional formula or creed (I Cor. 15:3b-7) which holds that
Jesus' rising on the third day was a fulfillment of prophecy.
Mark 8:31 reflects a similar tradition. In looking for a prophecy that three days after his burial Jesus' tomb would be empty,
the community apparently fastened upon a passage in Hosea:
" Come, let us return to the Lord; for he has torn, that he may
heal us; he has stricken, and he will bind us up. After two days
he will revive us; on the third day he will raise us up, that we
may live before him " (Hos. 6:1-2). Only by a stretch of the
imagination can this be taken as a prediction that three days
after his burial the tomb of Jesus would be empty because he
had risen from the dead. Yet early Christians, like their fellow
Jews, frequently used Scripture in this way both to achieve
and to reinforce their interpretation of events currently taking
place.

An empty grave vault, however, is scarcely conclusive evidence of a resurrection. The author of Matthew later recognized
this fact when he reported, only to reject, another current explanation for the disappearance of the body of Jesus from its
grave (Matt. 28:11-15). Yet Mark himself was evidently but

one among many who believed, on the evidence of reports concerning the empty tomb, that the resurrection had already taken place and that, therefore, they would shortly see Jesus. Mark's emphasis upon Galilee as the place where Jesus might be expected to show himself suggests that his Gospel may have been written shortly after A.D. 66–70, when in the face of Roman measures to suppress the Jewish revolt numerous refugees, including both Christians and Jews, had fled from Jerusalem to outlying provinces. In any case, he evidently shared with other disciples the belief that the crucified Jesus would soon disclose himself to them in Galilee (Mark 16:7). Yet these believers may well have been expecting of Jesus, not a brief appearance to confirm his resurrection, but his coming on the clouds of heaven as the Son of Man to consummate the Kingdom of God.[16]

Among the Synoptics, we find accounts of postcrucifixion appearances of Jesus, and incidentally also virgin birth legends, only in Matthew and Luke. Matthew preserves a tradition that Jesus appeared to the women as they ran from the graveyard to tell his disciples about the empty tomb (Matt. 28:9-10). If either Mark or Luke had heard of this tradition, each ignored it in writing his Gospel. The early creedal enumeration of postcrucifixion appearances in I Cor. 15:3b-7 also ignores this one to the women. Luke preserves an account of two disciples to whom Jesus appeared on the road to Emmaus. According to tradition, the two later reported that they themselves did not recognize Jesus, despite a long conversation with him concerning prophetic predictions of his sufferings, until finally at supper " he was known to them in the breaking of the bread " (Luke 24:13-53). Luke recounts a subsequent appearance in Jerusalem to the Eleven just as they were being told of the Emmaus experience. Matthew incorporates a tradition of a similar appearance to the Eleven on a mountain in Galilee, where in the midst of the experience some of the apostles themselves had doubts as to what was going on, though apparently they were convinced before the event was over (Matt. 28:16-20).

As an aside, it may be noted that Paul, in I Cor. 15:8, apparently regarded as equivalent to other postcrucifixion appearances his own experience on the Damascus road. Here again, reconstruction is difficult. The three extant accounts do not agree, for example, as to who heard and who did not hear the Voice from heaven (Acts 9:7; 22:9; 26:14).

Exploration of the origin and function of the resurrection narratives is made the more difficult by the cultural milieu out of which they arose. We have evidence that Herod Antipas, among others, was credited with believing that Jesus was John the Baptist raised from the dead (Mark 6:14-16 and parallels). Other traditions indicate that by some, Jesus was regarded as Elijah or another of the prophets raised from the dead (Mark 6:15; Luke 9:8; Mark 8:28 and parallels).

Historical reconstruction of the incidents of postcrucifixion appearance is obviously no longer possible solely upon the basis of evidence available in the kerygmatic material of the New Testament, and no other evidence is at hand. The impossibility of definitive historical reconstruction, however, does not render a theological reconstruction of these incidents entirely fruitless. If we can no longer determine exactly what happened in the resurrection experiences, we can still ask what meaning the experiences had for the early Christians, as evidenced in their preaching.

In the earliest Palestinian post-Easter preaching, the resurrection of Jesus functions in two ways — meaning by his resurrection, now, simply the empty tomb and the experiences, whatever they may have been, that underlay the accounts of his postcrucifixion appearances: (1) His resurrection thus experienced is pronounced the vindication of the life and preaching of Jesus. Thus it is claimed that what he said and did continues to be a valid diagnostic judgment and to pose a therapeutic crisis, despite his crucifixion. (2) The resurrection experiences are further adduced to evidence the secret enthronement of Jesus as the Messiah, the Son of God, the legitimate King of the nations; and to indicate the power and glory which will be his when, as the

Son of Man, he returns upon the clouds publicly to consummate the reign of God on earth.

Palestinian preaching a short time later had already begun, in the light of the resurrection experiences, to see in the crucifixion itself a preeminently probing diagnosis of human existence and a fateful prognosis, demanding of every man a choice between healing and death. In this stratum of preaching, the news is good, not in spite of the crucifixion, but because of it. The suffering and death of Jesus begin now to be seen in the perspective of Isa., ch. 53, and Jesus himself to be identified as the Suffering Servant of God.

EARLY CHRISTIAN PREACHING

In New Testament times there were evidently many people prepared both to accept — with no prejudice against their credibility — reports of the physical resurrection of the dead, and to entertain as plausible the idea that earth actually is invaded from time to time by manlike visitors (angels) from outer space. There is evidence that among such people the preaching of the crucified Jesus as the Christ, and the prediction of his imminent return as the Son of Man, often precipitated a crisis in self-understanding. This preaching sparked as well a therapeutic release of energies in a pattern of community (koinōnia) that quickly overreached the boundaries of nation, race, class, language, custom.

Viewed dynamically, this recurrent crisis in personal identity and the attendant release of energy in outreaching community is the expansion of a field of forces originating in the man Jesus. From this viewpoint, preaching appears as one of many elements in this energy complex. Viewed ideologically, the therapeutic release and reintegration precipitated by early Christian preaching appears to be a function of transmutations in traditional messianic concepts. These transmutations of the meanings of terms are consequent upon the recognition of Jesus as the Christ. From this perspective, preaching was the medium within which traditional messianism was transformed. In either view, the man Jesus stands historically at the center of the phenomena.

According to traditional conceptions, a man was the messiah of Yahweh only so long as he was physically present on earth. He exercised the authority and responsibility of government only within the Hebrew sociopolitical sphere. Only at the moment of his elevation into the institutional office did he become the son of God. He was king, therefore, not in the act of being himself a man, but in fulfilling an institutional role. Only as a king within the framework of the Davidic political dynasty, therefore, was an ancient Hebrew ever called " Wonderful Counselor, Mighty God, Everlasting Father, Prince of Peace " (Isa. 9:6).[17] Later Jewish idealizations of Davidic messianism, even when projecting the future realization of the Kingdom of Yahweh into another world than this one, never conceived of the coming scion of David in terms other than institutional.

The post-Easter proclamation of Jesus as the Christ broke the institutional frame of reference and called for his recognition as Messiah despite his physical absence. The language signifying his continued presence is metaphorical. Underlying these metaphors of presence is the perception (1) that the implications of his life and death are universal, reaching every man, (2) that these implications communicate themselves as there for us in symbolically concrete events such as preaching, the Sacraments of Baptism and Eucharist, the ecstasy of release, the transport of fellowship with believers. The meaning of his life and death for all men, stated metaphorically, is his already worldwide dominion, now at once concealed in concrete events and revealed through them to the eyes of faith. Early preaching presents as basic to this whole set of perceptions besides the public life and death of Jesus, his empty tomb, and his postcrucifixion appearances. His resurrection, therefore, could be perceived as itself the moment of his exaltation into Sonship and Messiahship. This point of view is expressed in an early creedal formula: " The gospel concerning his Son, who was descended from David according to the flesh and designated Son of God in power according to the Spirit of holiness by his resurrection from the dead, Jesus Christ our Lord " (Rom. 1:3-4). From the slightly changed perspective of Luke-Acts, the cessation of his post-crucifixion appearances and his ascension to heaven are viewed as the moment of his messianic exaltation. (Acts 1:9 ff.) The later Gospel of John even portrays the raising of Jesus on the cross as his elevation into Kingship. (John 12:28-34.)

On the other hand, from the perspective of the resurrection experiences, the early Palestinian Christians perceived the historical existence of Jesus as already implicitly messianic. But his exercise of messianic authority, according to the ideological model, implies his prior elevation into Kingship. The perception of this implication finds dramatic expression in the post-Easter stories which portray his baptism and transfiguration as enthronement events, at which he is elevated into his messiahship by the declaration of the Voice from heaven: " Thou art my beloved Son " (Mark 1:11 and parallels; cf. Mark 9:7, etc.).[18]

Matthew 11:25-27 and parallel in Luke 10:21-22, the single instance in the Synoptics representing Jesus as preexistently the Son of God, reflects an accommodation of Palestinian kerygma to Greek ways of thinking about the gods. On this view, Jesus was the eternal Son of God who humbled himself to become a man. The virgin birth stories, also found exclusively in Matthew and Luke, probably reflect a similar accommodation to Greek ways of thinking. On this view, Jesus was conceived as the Son of God, begotten by the Holy Spirit of the Virgin Mary.

The preaching of Jesus as Christ the King served to release and direct vast energies previously suppressed or inhibited by existing political establishments, to say nothing of a variety of other restrictive customs and institutions. His subjects saw themselves in the service of a king physically absent, conscripting no armies, levying no taxes, and yet secretly ruling all nations and peoples. Disciples but recently oppressed by Roman occupation, tyrannized by their own authorities, frustrated by their own blind hostility against all existing government, boldly demanded freedom of speech in the service of Jesus Christ and mounted civil and religious disobedience against authorities who refused it. Civil disobedience among Christians could and apparently did get out of hand, as evidenced by later injunctions to submit to governing authorities as unto God (Rom. 13:1-7; Titus 3:1; I Peter 2:13-17). Yet secular anarchy was not the aim of preaching Jesus as the Christ, for the release of revolutionary energies expected by this preaching was to be shaped and directed by an understanding of human existence specified in the preaching and conduct of the historical Jesus himself. Believers could resist when his work demanded, but no less boldly and freely they could bend the facilities even of the Roman Empire to the service of their King.

In New Testament preaching, the suffering and death of Jesus function in a wide variety of ways. In the earliest Palestinian kerygma, as we have seen, his passion had no positive significance. Only in the later strata of pre-Synoptic preaching is his suffering construed in the light of the servant passages in Isa., ch. 53. From this perspective, messianic and servant motifs were first fused to produce a portrait of Jesus as the Suffering Messiah, whose crucifixion itself exposes both the health and sickness of human existence — a health in which he risked death at the hands of those who were evidently threatened as much by the prospect of the health he offered as by his diagnosis of their condition. On this view, crucifixion becomes his most dramatic and extreme parable, expanding into action what earlier he had expressed in words: "Whoever seeks to gain his life will lose it, but whoever loses his life will preserve it."

At this level of New Testament preaching, the cross emerges as the preeminent symbol of health in the recurring human crisis. Health is served at the risk of personal loss; in extremity, death preferred to days lengthened at the cost of antitherapeutic existence. Yet the inevitable symbolic ambivalence of the cross conceals a double danger in the dynamics of being a Christian. The first is in the risk that one may overestimate his own health

and underestimate that of his neighbor and so become despoti-
cally messianic or Christian. The second is in the risk that one
may mistake passion itself as therapy and so become masochisti-
cally Christian, seducing his own destruction and brutalizing his
neighbor. Against these twin dangers New Testament preaching
offers as a checkpoint the preaching, life, and death of the historical Jesus.

The conception of Jesus as the Suffering Messiah, we have
noted is not an invention of the Synoptists. It is found already
in the Palestinian kerygmatic material upon which they drew.
The recognition of Jesus' death as a therapeutic event underlies
the post-Easter conversion of his words at the Last Supper. In
the revised account, he utters a eucharistic formula and com-
mands remembrance and symbolic reenactment of his atoning
sacrifice (Mark 14:22-24 and parallels). The perception of his
death as an atoning sacrifice in turn opened up the whole Temple cultus as a source of metaphors for use in preaching. Thus,
for example, Jesus was soon seen not only as the Son of God,
but as the sacrificial victim, the Paschal Lamb of God, whose
death removes the sins of the world.

Yet it should be observed that this particular institutionaliza-
tion, in Sacrament and metaphor, of the meaning of the cross of
Jesus tends completely to objectify the event. The costly up-
surge of healing energy through his crucifixion thus tends to appear as an occurrence wholly " out there," the like of which
need never occur in the individual. Jesus paid it all! From this
purely objectifying point of view, one can effectively discharge
the existential implications inherent in his preaching, life, and
death. In this way, Jesus can be idolized by those who refuse the
risk of being like him.

The earliest post-Easter preaching perceived the experience of
Jesus' resurrection as meaning that he was the one who would
soon return as the Son of Man, coming in glory on the clouds of
heaven. New Testament preaching never abandoned the hope
that the man Jesus himself would soon come back to earth, come
back to consummate the messianic judgment and redemption be-

gun in the humiliation and suffering of his first historical existence.

So intense is this hope in the Gospel of Mark, and so short the anticipated time, that the period between Easter and the Second Coming is virtually emptied of significance.

There is some evidence in the Lucan accounts that the very preaching of this hope, itself, occasioned a therapeutic transformation of human relationships within the early church. Believers in Jerusalem sold their possessions, pooled the proceeds, and devised communal arrangements under which each contributed according to his ability and received according to his need. The consequent new vision of the neighbor and the emergence of love (*agapē*) within community were proclaimed as the work of the Spirit of the Lord Christ himself. Incidental dishonesty, preferential treatment, and dissension over the handling of funds were attributed to the spirit of the devil. A socialist economy for the consumption of capital goods, however, could not survive a long delay of the second coming. The unexpected prolongation of time, the stubborn persistence of the present world, required of love new modes of understanding and new kinds of expression.

Matthew and Luke provide evidence of mounting anxiety over the delay of Jesus' second coming and a consequent return to his significance for the here and now. The interpretation placed by Jesus himself upon his own preaching and behavior stressed, of course, implications for present decision. Nor is any later stratum of New Testament preaching devoid of existential implication. But the delay of the second coming clearly intensified questions as to his significance for decision in the present. While we can no longer trace the steps by which these questions were concretely raised and answered, we can observe definite changes in the way basic kerygmatic concepts were used, and consequent shifts in their meaning.

Matthew 25:31-46, to take but one example, preserves from a late stratum of Synoptic preaching a sermon. This sermon deals ostensibly with the coming of the Son of Man in glory, attended

by angels, sitting on his royal throne to judge the nations at the
end of the age. The preacher first has the Messianic King speak
to those on his right and then to those on his left, saying to the
latter: " Depart from me, you cursed, into the eternal fire prepared for the devil and his angels; for I was hungry and you gave
me no food, I was thirsty and you gave me no drink, I was a
stranger and you did not welcome me, naked and you did not
clothe me, sick and in prison and you did not visit me." A second look at the way this language is used, however, makes quite
clear that the preacher is talking about a confrontation here and
now, and a judgment going on in this present world. For the
condemned demand of the King, " When did we see thee hungry or thirsty or a stranger or naked or sick or in prison, and did
not minister to thee? " And the reply comes back, " As you did
it not to one of the least of these, you did it not to me." Ask on
the basis of this sermon, " How do I recognize Christ my judge
and king in this present time? " and the answer is, " He is your
neighbor in need."

The Easter experiences recede more and more into the past.
Delay of the second coming is daily prolonged. The present
world won't go away. In these circumstances, the themes of Jesus' resurrection and second coming were not abandoned in
preaching. But in treating of their relevance for the time being,
New Testament preaching itself began a transformation of the
meaning of the themes.

Signs of Judgment and Healing

Critical research upon the New Testament is precipitating a
new crisis in Christian faith. The shape of that crisis appears in
summarizing the more recent findings of critical study.

Belief in Jesus as the Christ and the expectation of his imminent return as the coming Son of Man arose only after Easter,
on the evidence of the New Testament itself. The identification
of Jesus as the coming Son of Man implies that the completed
shape of human history has already been foreshadowed in his

own prior historical existence. This belief emerged around what may be called the experiences of Jesus' resurrection. His resurrection was preached as the basic indication that this very Jesus is the one appointed to return as the Son of Man. Delay of his second coming precipitated a major (and still enduring) crisis in Christian faith. The extension of time and the persistence of this world put in question the present significance of the answer: He was raised from the dead and is coming again.

New Testament preaching, as we have seen, evidences the perception that the authentic pattern of human existence was originally fulfilled in Jesus and will be fulfilled again in others. The prolongation of time in this world raises the possibility that belief in his second coming simply interprets that perception in apocalyptic language. Where, after all, if not in persons, can the authentic shape of human historical existence come to completion? Furthermore, the impossibility of a historical reconstruction of the Easter event, upon the basis of the only accounts available, has led to the suspension of judgment as to the historicity of Jesus' resurrection. Yet this does not mean that his resurrection dissolves into sheer believing — a " faith event." New Testament statements about Easter refer to the resurrection of the historical Jesus. In effect, therefore, propositions about both his resurrection and his second coming function for the time being, not as accounts of supranatural miracles past and future, but as statements about generalized patterns or meanings of human existence in this world — patterns first discerned in the man Jesus, and later observed within the fellowship of his disciples.

The new quest for the historical Jesus has made evident that New Testament preaching was responsive, not only to memories of Jesus, but to the actual words in which he interpreted his own work. Clearly, he saw both his own preaching and his personal behavior as elements in a diacritical and therapeutic event. We next turn to the logically consequent question. In the postcrucifixion era, where did the Christian community perceive the authentic pattern of human existence recurrently fulfilled? What kind of human behavior signaled for them the same sort of diagnosis and therapy going on in the current time?

We shall briefly examine three New Testament answers. For the purpose of this brief survey, we shall bracket in these three answers propositions about the supranatural resurrection and second coming of Jesus, except as they bear directly upon the original author's discernment of healing in the present time. For we have indicated that all propositions relative to Jesus' resurrection and second coming function for the time being as statements about generalized patterns of human existence perceived as originally and concretely occurring in him and in this world.

Christian religiosity emerges as the sign of present salvation in The Letter to the Hebrews. Yet, curiously, the argument of the book would seem to point to a different conclusion.

This work was written in time of persecution. It is generally dated not earlier than A.D. 75–80, hence after the fall of Jerusalem and the destruction of the Temple in A.D. 70. Conceivably, the work was addressed to disillusioned Essenes and others who, until the destruction of the Temple, had shared the hope of a coming Priestly Messiah in the succession of Aaron. If, however, the author is presenting Jesus as the transformation and fulfillment of those hopes, he does so without once referring to prior expectations of a Priestly Messiah or once using the phrase itself.

The author understands heaven to be the realm of indestructible originals, and earth the place of unenduring imitations. He imagines, therefore, a temple and a cultus in heaven of which the Jerusalem Temple and its cultus is but a copy and a shadow. (Heb. 8:5.) Thus he wraps around the resurrection of Jesus and his second coming another layer of imaginary events, offering the reader a conceptual system, the function of which must be examined as a whole.

He supposes, upon the basis of Ps. 2:7 and 110:4, that Jesus was the preexistent Son of God, appointed the high priest of heaven's sanctuary (Heb. 5:5-6; 7:15-16). The author recognizes that Jesus was descended from Judah in his bodily existence, and thus was not a member of any earthly order of priests. (Ch. 7:14.) But on the author's understanding, the Aaronite-Levitical priesthood is another of the imperfect copies — a priestly order in which no man can permanently hold office because he has to die (chs. 7:11, 23; 8:5). Continuing his curious exegesis of Ps. 110:4, he holds that Jesus, by virtue of his indestructible life as the Son of God (Heb. 7:16), is " a priest for ever, after the order of Melchizedek." The Levitical blood offerings, therefore, were imperfect and repetitive foreshadowings, inefficacious of themselves. Jesus, on the other hand, " appeared once for all at the end of the age to put away sin by the sacrifice of himself," a perfect and efficacious offering which need never and could never be repeated (chs. 9:25-26; 10:12-14). The earthly temple, the old covenant, the Aaronite priesthood, are all now obsolete, for Jesus has established a new covenant in his blood, has been raised from the dead, and taking his humanity with him has reascended into heaven's sanctuary, whence he will soon appear a second time to save those who eagerly await his coming (chs. 8 and 9).

From this point of view, present salvation is faith, or existential belief, in Jesus as the Son of God (Heb. 3:12-16), and the indispensable sign of salvation is the assembly of believers for worship (chs. 10:25-31; 4:15-16). Put another way, the preaching and confession of Jesus as the Word of God is the indispensable historical sign of crisis and therapy in the time being (ch. 4:11-13). The essential sacrifice here and now is verbal and ideological. (Ch. 13:15.)

For the author of Hebrews, therefore, Jesus is not the Son and Word of God in the sense that the pattern of a generalized therapeutic energy is perceptible in his life and death. The book portrays, not a functional, but a substantival understanding of therapy. The matter could be put this way: Jesus is the preexistent and indestructible " I " of God himself, in the mode of self-utterance, who has taken flesh, died, and risen again to bring into the life of God the humanity he assumed and saved. Similarly, the text exhibits, not a functional, but a substantival understanding of mortal men. Thus, every man except Jesus is seen as a created " I," who has (not who is) a mind and body. From this perspective, only one man has ever existed and that one man is Jesus the Son of God. All other " men " are evanescent shadows whose only hope lies in what he has done and will do for all who believe in him. Viewed as a statement produced in a period of persecution, this austere interpretation of history is psychologically intelligible. Yet its messianism largely robs of meaning all history except that of the man Jesus perceived as the Son of God. Thus what seemed at first to be an argument that no particular historical cultus is indispensable to hygienic human existence turns out on close inspection to be an argument that there is no health, no manhood, outside the Jesus cult. Not surprisingly, a few believers seem to have lost interest (ch. 10:25).

Conceivably, the author of Hebrews intended the imagery of his preexistential and apocalyptic language to be taken as poetry. Whether or not he so intended, critical study of the New Testament suggests the possibility of viewing his whole conceptual system as a poetic statement about human existence perceived in relation to the life and death of Jesus.

When viewed as poetry, the language about heavenly originals and earthly copies affirms that essence precedes existence. In other words, a man's authentically humane possibilities are declared to be there prior to the decision in which they are expressed or defaulted. Jesus then becomes the concrete case in which essence and existence are seen to coincide. He chose his most proper and authentically human possibilities under the particular circumstances of his life and death. His crucifixion, therefore, evokes decision for the most authentically human possibility within every other man under the unrepeatable circumstances of his own space and time. This evocation is the priestly office of Jesus. For the author of The Letter to the Hebrews, moreover, the most generalized form of the authentically human is existence in faith. And faith he conceives as decision here and now, in the light of the past, for the possibility coming out of the future.

When his work is taken as poetry, however, faith has two aspects which should be carefully noted. First, existence in faith is viewed in detachment from the psychosomatic processes apart from which it does not occur. The historic is disjoined from the historical. The believer sees himself and his neighbor as disembodied subjectivity. He views his world as a wasteland, a wilderness en route to a promised land into which he never comes. The call to exist by faith, as here understood, means being reconciled to radical estrangement. Second, in this letter faith is perceived in no organic relation with ethical behavior. Brotherly love is commanded. But faith, not brotherly love, is viewed as the miracle of God in man. The believer is called to endure injustice and martyrdom for his faith; but he is never exhorted to resist evil or to overcome it, even on behalf of the injured neighbor. He has no responsibility for orders of justice in earthly cities. He opts out of responsibility in the here and now by seeking a heavenly city. His New Jerusalem is always coming but never anywhere even fragmentarily arriving, except in the cultus of verbal confession and praise of Jesus as the pioneer and paradigm of faith. Again, however, we are reminded that The Letter to the Hebrews is the poetry of faith foreshortened by persecution, a poetry that does not encompass the full vision of the tradition upon which it depends.

The fruits of the Spirit appear as the sign of salvation in the present age according to the apostle Paul. Early in his missionary career (ca. A.D. 50), he was preaching the resurrection and imminent second coming of Jesus in quite prosaic imagery (I Thess. 1:10). The converts at Thessalonica seem to have understood such apocalyptic language even more prosaically than did Paul. He later felt called upon to allay anxiety concerning those believers who had died before the Lord's return. He assured Thessalonian readers that, far from being left out of the great event, the dead would have a leading role in it. Only when the dead had first been raised would the living be caught up into the air with them to meet the returning Lord. (I Thess. 4:13-18.) There is no evidence that Paul ever abandoned this most

unpoetical use of apocalyptic imagery. He could and did, therefore, speak of justification by faith in language quite similar to
that later used in The Letter to the Hebrews.

On the other hand, as the second coming was delayed he began to write to his living converts in clearly poetical fashion of
a death and resurrection that they had already undergone. Thus,
to the Christians in Rome: " Do you not know that all of us who
have been baptized into Christ Jesus were baptized into his
death? We were buried therefore with him by baptism into death,
so that as Christ was raised from the dead by the glory of the
Father, we too might walk in newness of life." (Rom. 6:3-4.)
Believers here on earth have already been raised from the dead,
and their new life for the time being is hid with Christ in God.
(Col. 2:1-3.)

Paul places these poetic interpretations of death and resurrection within the framework of his prosaic apocalypticism. " When
Christ who is our life appears, then you also will appear with
him in glory." (Col. 3:4; cf. Rom. 6:8-10.) Often, as in this
case, no details are specified. Even when he supplies specifica-
tions, they do not actually specify. He declares firmly, for example, that a man's flesh and blood are not preserved in the processes of the divine life — i.e., flesh and blood do not enter
heaven (I Cor. 15:50). Man is raised a spiritual *sōma*. (V. 44.)
But a spiritual somatics having really nothing to do with flesh
and blood is utterly beyond our ken. Effectively, therefore, even
his apocalyptic resurrection imagery signifies a mode of historic
existence in the present time.

This new " existence here and now " can be viewed either as
Christ living in the believer or as the believer living in Christ.
Thus Paul can say of himself: " I have been crucified with
Christ; it is no longer I who live, but Christ who lives in me "
(Gal. 2:20). On the other hand, he can declare that any man
who is " in Christ " is a new creation (II Cor. 5:17); or he can
announce that " in Christ Jesus " all believers are sons of God
through faith (Gal. 3:26). Being raised from the dead, in this
usage, is the poetic equivalent of existence in Christ.

Paul does not directly and concretely specify the shape of this hidden existence in Christ. He does, however, detail the signs of existence in the Spirit (*Pneuma*). Through the latter conception, it is possible to glimpse obliquely what he regarded as present signs that believers here and now have already been raised from the dead and are now hiddenly existing in Christ.

As he speaks of Christ, so also he speaks of the Spirit as that within which the believer exists (Rom. 8:9), and that which dwells in the believer (I Cor. 3:16). Indeed, the indwelling of the Spirit of God and the having of the Spirit of Christ are clearly, for him, obverse faces of a single phenomenon (Rom. 8:9-11). He can even say, " The Lord is the Spirit " (II Cor. 3:17), with probable reference to Jesus. Hence, to have Christ's Spirit is to have the Spirit of God. To be in Christ is to be in the Spirit.

What indications have we, then, as to the differences arising here and now from life in the Spirit? Noteworthy at this point is the fact that Paul, like the later author of The Letter to the Hebrews, views God and man substantively, rather than functionally. He discusses Spirit phenomena, therefore, not simply in terms of the structure and dynamics of their occurring, but as productions caused by an imaginary producer, work done by an unseen worker. Thus for him the signs of therapy in the here and now are the firstfruits produced by the Spirit in the believer (Rom. 8:23). His description of these fruits both delineates a mode of self-understanding and behavior, and implies a distinctive world view. The fruits of the Spirit are love, joy, patience, forgiveness, fidelity, compassion, humility, self-control, and the like. (Cf. Gal. 5:22-23; Col. 3:12-14.) Opposed to the Spirit and its fruits (*karpos*) are the flesh (*sarx*) and its works (*erga*). Flesh in this usage does not mean the physical body, but the demonic antitype of Spirit. Its works both constitute a contrasting mode of self-understanding and behavior, and imply an opposing world view. The works of the flesh are fornication, lasciviousness, carousing, idolatry, sorcery, lying, malice, contentiousness, jealousy, vengeful wrath, self-promotion, divisiveness, partisanship, envy, and the like. (Cf. Gal. 5:19-21; Col. 3:5-9.)

For Paul however, existence in the Spirit is ecstatic. Our recognition of God as " Papa " (*Abba*) is God's recognition of himself through the Spirit of his Son indwelling us. (Gal. 4:6.) Healing ecstasy is a resurrection and an ascension into a dialogue internal to God, an eternal communion (*koinōnia*). Thus he can speak of Jesus Christ as the one who " brought life and immortality to light " (II Tim. 1:10).

Paul sees the fruits of the Spirit, therefore, as charismata. His encomium of love (*agapē*) in I Cor., ch. 13, for example, is not a tribute to self-made lovers. To read Paul and say to oneself, " I will go love my neighbor in order to be authentic," is entirely to miss his point. For to love either the self or the neighbor for the sake of being authentic is to love neither the self nor the neighbor at all. The love he celebrates in men is at once a rapture and a charisma, the highest and most excellent gift of the Spirit (I Cor. 12:31). Love as he sees it can be inhibited or repressed. It can be invited or evoked, but never produced or manufactured. Its minimal manifestation always draws a man out of himself toward the world and the neighbor. At least in that sense love is always ecstatic. Because Paul sees the undiminished endowment bestowed, not only upon the man Jesus but upon others as well, the expression of love is for him an extensive and recurrent historical possibility. By the grace of God, it can happen here and now! Furthermore, for Paul, faith, hope, and love are the only present therapeutic phenomena that will survive unchanged into the time of the Lord's coming. " So faith, hope, love abide, these three; but the greatest of these is love." (I Cor. 13:13.)

God is love and love is the sign of human renewal according to the Johannine literature. In this fusion of God and sign, Johannine theology begins to approximate a purely functional description of salvation, in which the name of God and the name for what God does, with appropriate qualification, become interchangeable terms.

The Prologue of the Fourth Gospel approaches the significance of Jesus in terms of a conception of the Word (*Logos*) of God. The nuances of this expression in Greek usage are but faintly intimated in translation. In the first place, " word " and cognate terms in English tend to underscore the verbal aspects of speaking and thinking. *Logos* and *logikos,* by contrast, emphasize as well that logicality of processes and objects which both determines what they are and enables them to be thought. Thus biology, psychology, musicology, and like terms ending in -logy (from *logos*) clearly constitute a species of thinking and speaking about life — the psyche, music, and the like — while at the same time they purport to signify as well the logic (from *logikos*), for example, of the actual processes and behavior of the psyche.

A more specific illustration of the Greek outlook upon the dimensions of the logical is provided by the technical term *logos spermatikos,* spermatic or seminal logic. Current alike in popular and academic Greek science of the New Testament period and earlier, this expression denotes among other things the internal logic or " instructions " determining the development of organisms, each after its own kind. (By reason of its *seminal logic,* e.g., an acorn develops into nothing else than an oak bearing acorns capable of the same sort of development.) Compare with all this the idea, current today, that the organic development of the ontogenetic individual is determined by specific arrangements encoded within the molecular structure of DNA (deoxyribonucleic acid), a basic determinant of all living cell formation.

The author of the Prologue may have been influenced by Greek thought only indirectly through his dependence upon Hebrew Wisdom Literature. There is no evidence for or against his familiarity with the conception of spermatic logic prevalent in the Greek science of his day. Yet his account of the divine *logos* is illumined by Greek scientific terminology then current, and has even stronger affinities with more general usage of the term in Greek philosophy. What sharply distinguishes the Prologue from the Greek manner of thinking emerges in the declaration that the divine *logos* became flesh — was encoded, so to speak, in the life of the particular man Jesus.

> In the beginning was the Logic,
>   and the Logic was with God,
>   and the Logic was God.
> He was in the beginning with God;
>   all things were made through him,
>   and without him was not anything made that
>   was made. . . .
> And the Logic became flesh
>   and dwelt among us, full of grace and truth.
> (Translating *Logos* as " Logic," John 1:1-3, 14.)

Before we examine the therapeutic dimensions of this event, it is well to observe that in the Prologue the concept " man " implicitly functions as a double-hyphenated term, at once correlative to the concept of God (*Theos*) and to the concept of world (*kosmos*). We have here a theandrocosmic (God-man-world) point of view in which the term " God " first names the mystery of man and his world. The Fourth Gospel shares with the whole New Testament the understanding that even in the Jesus event man has neither a direct vision of God nor any comprehension of the divine mystery as such. We have no clue to the depths of the ultimate mystery of man and his world other than the expression fathered by the mystery itself. " No one has ever seen God; the only begotten God [*monogenēs Theos*], who is in the bosom of the Father, he has made him known." (John 1:18, accepting the text as it appears in three of our earliest manuscripts.) Yet the mystery is self-uttered, has spoken to us. " And the Word was God."

Nothing, however, is really affirmed in saying that " the Word was God " unless it can be also said in some sense that God was the Word. Yet the latter proposition must always be strictly qualified. God is the Word only in the revelatory situation — only in going out toward what is not God. What God, as the mystery of man and his cosmos, may be outside the revelatory relationship is for us quite unknowable in the nature of the case.

Even Jesus is no incarnation of the unuttered mystery. Yet within the revelatory situation, he is declared to be the one in whom is encoded or incarnate that *Logos* which is God's utterance of himself for us.

The Prologue, however, sees human existence to be largely divorced from the manifest logic of its own mystery. The Word of God came forth unrecognized by the very world that the divine logic informs, a stranger amid the very people whose life and light the *Logos* is. Yet he enabled those who did receive him to become sons (*tekna*) of God, children born " not of blood nor of the flesh nor of the will of man, but of God." (Ch. 1:4-14.) Thus in the man Jesus the logic of human existence precipitated a continuing crisis from which eventuate here and now, either light, healing, and life or darkness, morbidity, and death. (Ch. 3:18-21.)

Therapy and life, approached in the Prologue in terms of the incarnation of the divine Word, are viewed elsewhere in the Johannine literature as also the work of the Spirit of God, a new movement of the divine Breath through human history (John 14:17; 16:13-15; I John 3:24 to 4:3; 4:13). For God is *Pneuma* (Breath) (John 4:24) as well as Word, in the sense that the divine self-expression among us is a dynamic no less than a structured event. Thus Jesus' initiation into his messianic role is represented, for example, by the Spirit's descending upon him (John 1:32), and the abundant life he brings as made available only by rebirth of the Spirit of God (John 3:3-8).

An innovative element in Johannine theology is its movement away from substantival toward functional description of the theandric healing event. This originality climaxes in The First Letter of John. To the question whether or not healing is going on, I John proposes a clear and present sign. " We know that we have passed out of death into life, because we love." (I John 3:14.) Yet love is more. For in I John the Johannine viewpoint is pressed to its logical conclusion. Love here becomes for man at once the sign of life and the sign of God, " for God is love " (I John 4:8). Love is preeminently the messianic event in the time being. The question then arises as to the way in which God is that love which signals the healing of man.

I John 4:7-8 provides an almost perfect paradigm for the concrete and specific identification of God in human life here and now. Analyzing the phenomenon of love (*agapē*), the author first observes that love is of God. This is not to deny that the act of love is man's own act. It is, rather, to identify the capacity for love as a charisma, a divine endowment, the encoded logic by virtue of which existence is theandrocosmic rather than exclusively anthropological. It follows that the man who actually loves is a theocosmic function; he is a specific and concrete moment in the divine dialogue or intercourse. In the poetry of I John, he " is born of God and knows God." The man who does not actually love has no such intercourse, " does not know God." In him theandrocosmic communion and communication are broken. Here two things are made clear, as they are also made clear in the Prologue of the Fourth Gospel: First, that the healing renewal of theandrocosmic communion pivots around the event Jesus Christ. Second, that God appears in this healing action, not as he is in himself, but as he is in human history — that is to say, as love. " For God is love." (V. 8.) " No man has ever seen God; if we love one another, God abides in us and his love is perfected [historically completed] in us." (V. 12.) Or the summation can be made another way. " God is love, and he who abides in love abides in God, and God abides in him." (V. 16.)

Theologians who readily admit the proposition that " God is love," often declare invalid the obverse statement that " love is God." Yet under the conditions of history, what the New Testament denotes as love is identically God, or else the Johannine proposition that God is love means actually nothing at all.

This almost perfect Johannine paradigm is flawed, however, in one respect, namely, by an apparently diminished conception of the role of *agapē* in the time being. This judgment is not grounded simply in a private preference for some other conception of *agapē* to be found elsewhere in the New Testament. The judgment arises from the apparent failure of the whole Johan-

nine tradition to abide by the consequences of its own decision
— the decision, namely, to take the love manifest in Jesus as the
prototypical standard by which to determine whether divine
agapē is completed in any subsequent historical action. Writers
in this tradition repeatedly declare that in Jesus Christ the divine love reaches out to the entire world. (John 3:16-18, 36;
4:9-10; 6:40; cf. Rev. 3:20.) Yet they characteristically portray
the operation of that love in the believer as extending particu-
larly toward those of the ingroup. By way of illustration: " We
know that we have passed out of death into life, because we love
the brethren " (I John 3:14; cf. chs. 3:16; 4:20; John 17:6-
26). It is also characteristic of this tradition neither to affirm nor
to deny the possibility and demand for the historical realization
of *agapē* between enemies. In other respects it can be shown
that the implications of the Christ event are better glimpsed
elsewhere in the New Testament, insofar as those implications
deal with the possibility of recurrent completion (*teleiosis*) of divine love in concrete actions of men. The portrayal of love is
fuller, for example, in the Sermon on the Mount (Matt. 5:43-
48) and I Cor., ch. 13.

We have called attention to the hermeneutic procedures by
which the Johannine paradigm was derived. The original Johannine authors themselves first interpreted resurrection and
apocalyptic language as poetic declarations of the prototypical
significance of the man Jesus for every man in the world for the
time being. The author of I John next perceived that God,
within the limits of the androcosmic scene, is identically the
therapeutic process universalized in Jesus. This perception reflects the interpretation of the Word of God in the Prologue of
the Fourth Gospel.

Adopting this method of interpretation, we might revisit The
Letter to the Hebrews, as well as the Pauline and Johannine literature, to make explicit what stands only implicitly in their
various accounts of judgment and healing in the time being. Following this method, we might reinterpret existence in faith (*pis-
tis*), which occurs in the salvation event at once as an act of God

and as an act of the believer, according to New Testament interpretation. Or we might reexamine the conception of community (*koinōnia*) in Pauline literature, to discover that specific
forms of community are identically God manifest. The possibilities are quite numerous.

Perhaps more germane to our present historical situation is
Paul's interpretation of God's act in Jesus Christ as the reintegrating (*katallassō*) of the world with himself (II Cor. 5:19).
From this point of view, God's action in the believer constitutes
a ministry of reintegration (*katallagē*). Thus, following the procedures underlying our paradigm, we can observe still another
way in which God identifies himself among men. God is the reintegration of fragmented human existence. We can then quite
properly infer, without violence to the announced intentions of
Paul, that within the conditions of history the authentic reintegration of fragmented human existence is identically and mani-
festly God. The New Testament characteristically tests specific
reintegrative action against the integrative Spirit and logic operative in the Jesus event. Reintegration is false insofar as it
exhibits another spirit or a less universal logic.

Here again, the Pauline perception of the dynamic logic of
the Jesus event is clearer than the Johannine. He speaks of God's
work in Christ as the reintegrating of the world with himself.
Paul's imperative: " Be integrated with God " (v. 20) is thus a
call to exhibit in action a unity that constitutes already the encoded logic of human existence even before man acts toward the
neighbor in his world. Exactly that prior encoded unity enables
us, first, to recognize fragmentation and distortion for what they
are, both in the private and in the public sphere of action, and
then to work and hope for historical reintegration despite the
phenomena of alienation and segregation. Through Christ, according to Paul, God reintegrated with himself, not mankind
alone, but all things whatsoever, whether on earth or in heaven;
" in him all things hold together " (Col. 1:17 ff.). Thus Paul
could approach any situation, however fragmented or distorted,
with confidence that the hidden healing logic of God works al-

ready within its energies — with the knowledge, moreover, that a like fragmentation and healing operate within himself and his own institutions. The Fourth Gospel, by contrast, celebrates a unity inclusive only of believers, and enjoins toward the world a hostility (cf. John, ch. 17) in sharp contrast with the love which God himself is elsewhere declared to have toward it (ch. 3:16).

Epilogue

Neither Pauline nor Johannine thought fully develops a theology of messianic existence in the time being. The development is cut short by persistence of belief that the world we know will be destroyed by extrinsic forces, possibly quite soon. Yet the foundations are here laid for a new messianic theology concerned with existence in the time being. Though its implications stand often unextrapolated, they are clearly established. The new messianism views the present condition of man as at once tragic and divinely comic, the occasion both for sadness and for mirth and joy.

The Pauline and Johannine theologies alike express a profound sense of man's ambiguity and ambivalence. Each regards human imagination as a double agent, capable of destroying a man or of saving him, depending upon his inspiration. Each understands that inspired and creative ecstasy looks, Janus-faced, in two directions. Each knows that man's inspirations impel him as readily to diminish as to enlarge the creative process. Both identify as the primary creative enterprise of man, human existence itself — the project in which each man undertakes to be what in some sense he is given to be. Both find in the double edge of creativity the source at once of the grandeur and of the misery of man. For human creativity, when directed against its own sources, dehumanizes men and encodes a logic of annihilation. Thus the basic human tragedy is identified as pathological existence, in which potentialities for life are turned against themselves — impaired existence, in which powers of existential sanity operate obscurely within shapes of morbidity and death.

Both theologies further imply that historic social orders and value systems are flawed by their pathogenic sources in man himself. In this respect, man's world, his objectified creations, need healing no less than does man himself, the creative subject. Under the delusion of the imminent world's end, New Testament apocalypticism often attempts a radical rejection of all secular orders, and enjoins for the time being a truncated existence amounting to social parasitism and irresponsibility. Paul in particular has largely overcome this irresponsible otherworldliness, yet without absolutizing the concrete value systems within which he lived. In fact, such Pauline and Johannine conceptions as *koinōnia, agapē,* and *zōē* serve implicitly both as presuppositions for responsible social criticism and as guidelines for reconstructing secular systems and institutions. They indicate as well the immanent therapeutic resources that enable such criticism and renewal of social order.

Both theologies celebrate a present release of healing energies stemming from the advent and reception of Jesus as the Christ. For both theologies, he is uniquely the Messiah, the Son of God. The Gospel of John, for example, acknowledges the ancient tradition in which the prince was considered a god. (See John 10.34 in comment upon Ps. 82:6.) Jesus is acknowledged, however, as the preeminent Son of God. He is the Messiah, the God-man, moreover, not by virtue of institutional office, but in the very act of being a man. Though he is deemed to be Alpha and Omega, the beginning and the end, he is not considered the only specimen of his kind. He is seen, rather, as the firstborn among many brethren (Rom. 8:29). Beyond his being the historic original of the new man, his preeminence lies in this: that his stature measures the fullness of messianic existence (cf. Eph. 4:13). His part in his crucifixion is viewed as a consummately therapeutic act, unclouded by any ambiguity. His living and dying alike are seen to manifest the charisma of healing in perfect clarity. More than that no messiah can do or be.

The therapeutic energies perceived and celebrated in Jesus as the Christ are seen to be operative as well in the time being.

These energies, moreover, are portrayed as neither extrinsic nor alien to man. To all who believe is given power to become children of God. (Cf. John 1:12.) "And if children, then heirs, heirs of God and fellow heirs with Christ, provided we suffer with him in order that we may also be glorified with him." (Rom. 8:17.) Inferentially, godmanhood is potential in every encounter of man with man. Messianic existence has become a recurrent possibility for every man, provided only that he is trusting and willing enough to pay the price of therapeutic existence in a world that often resembles nothing so much as a madhouse. "Perfect love casts out fear." (I John 4:18.) But our sickness is that we are afraid both to love and to be loved. Our recovery depends upon a miracle that can happen only in the presence of another like ourselves. If we may borrow from another context one of Luther's rare and felicitous phrases, the meaning of messianic existence for Pauline and Johannine theology, then, implicitly is this: that in the time being "we are alternately and mutually Christ one to another" (*invicem mutuoque sumus alter alterius Christus*).[19] The coming and reception of the Christ, however, is never a man's achievement out of himself but is, rather, a divine charisma, the reincarnation of God, a spontaneous endowment to be feared and denied or to be trusted and exercised.

Notes

Chapter I. MESSIANIC KINGSHIP IN ANCIENT ISRAEL

1. The term "messianic" as applied to Hebrew kings is used here to signify "in reference to the anointed." Compare the usage of Gerhard von Rad, *Old Testament Theology,* Vol. I (Harper & Brothers, 1962), p. 316, n. 13. "Messiah" simply anglicizes the Hebrew word *mashiach.* Contrast Sigmund Mowinckel, *He That Cometh,* tr. by G. W. Anderson (Abingdon Press, 1956), p. 3 and nn. 1 and 2, and also pp. 99, 101, and 123, who, against Gressman, Gunkel, Sellin, Jeremias, Staerk, and others, rejects the use of "messianic" in reference to the Hebrew kings, because of the lack of a technical eschatology in Oriental kingship ideology. The argument is revived by Aubrey R. Johnson, *Sacral Kingship in Ancient Israel* (Cardiff: University of Wales Press Board, 1955), p. 54, n. 1, and pp. 133 ff.

2. For the literature on sacral kingship in the ancient Near East as it relates to Hebrew monarchy, see Mowinckel, *op. cit.,* Ch. III, and G. von Rad, *Old Testament Theology,* Vol. I, p. 321, n. 6.

3. Cf. G. von Rad, *Old Testament Theology,* Vol. I, pp. 93 ff.

4. Cf. *ibid.,* p. 331, n. 7. See also Martin Noth, *The History of Israel,* 2d ed., tr. rev. by P. R. Ackroyd (London: Adam & Charles Black, Ltd., 1960), pp. 101–103.

5. Compare Murray Newman, "The Prophetic Call of Samuel," in *Israel's Prophetic Heritage,* ed. by B. W. Anderson and Walter Harrelson (Harper & Brothers, 1962), who argues for the possibility that the tradition which makes Samuel the transitional figure from covenant mediator to classical prophet may well preserve an authentic historical memory.

Though he is not responsible for my views, I welcome this opportunity to acknowledge my debt to Professor Newman's stimulating picture of the theological situation in Israel at the rise of the monarchy. See his *The People of the Covenant: A Study of Israel from Moses to the*

Monarchy (Abingdon Press, 1962).

6. Cf. G. von Rad, *Old Testament Theology,* Vol. I, p. 321, n. 6.

7. Cf. *ibid.,* pp. 132–135, 166 ff., 187 ff.

8. Cf. *ibid.,* p. 40, n. 4, and p. 310, n. 4.

9. Cf. *ibid.,* pp. 310 ff.

10. See *ibid.,* p. 348, n. 4, but contrast Johnson, *op. cit.,* p. 101, n. 2.

11. For the literature of the controversy, see Johnson, *op. cit.,* p. 23, n. 2; Mowinckel, *op. cit.,* p. 100, n. 3. Gerhard von Rad holds to the priority of II Sam., ch. 7, but finds in Ps. 89:20-30 very ancient traditions, *Old Testament Theology,* Vol. I, p. 310, n. 5.

12. The poet's use of the strange figure of the lamp should be compared with the Deuteronomist's use of the same figure in I Kings 11:36; 15:4; II Kings 8:19. Cf. G. von Rad, *Old Testament Theology,* Vol. I, p. 341, n. 18.

13. Cf. *ibid.,* p. 311, n. 8.

14. For the literature on the enthronement psalms, see G. von Rad, *Old Testament Theology,* Vol. I, p. 363, n. 14, where note is made of the dispute as to the number of psalms within the genre. He lists as most certainly within it, Ps. 47; 93; 96; 97; 98; 99. To these, Johnson, in *Sacral Kingship,* adds a number of others, including Ps. 29; 48; 68; 84; 95.

15. The translation is that of Johnson, *op. cit.,* p. 100.

16. For the literature on the royal psalms, see Johnson, *op. cit.,* p. 6, n. 1. As certainly belonging to the class, G. von Rad lists Ps. 2; 18; 20; 21; 45; 72; 89; 101; 110; and 132; cf. *Old Testament Theology,* p. 319, n. 1.

17. Ps. 2:2; 18:50; 20:6; 89:38; 132:10, 17.

18. On divine sonship in the whole of the ancient Near East, cf. G. von Rad, *Old Testament Theology,* Vol. I, p. 320, n. 4; but note Mowinckel's comment on the misplaced legend concerning Samuel's birth as a suppressed idea of Saul's prenatal election; cf. *He That Cometh,* p. 67, n. 1.

19. Cf. Ps. 2; 18:43 f.; 72:8-11; 89:25-27.

20. For the more dramatic statement of this ancient idea by the Chronicler after the expiration of the monarchy, see G. von Rad in reference to I Chron. 28:5; 29:23, etc., *Old Testament Theology,* Vol. I, p. 320, n. 5, and p. 350.

21. For this and what immediately follows, cf. *Old Testament Theology,* Vol. I, pp. 371–373.

22. Cf. *ibid.,* p. 374, especially von Rad's comment on Gen. 38:26.

23. For some of the literature, cf. Mowinckel, *op. cit.,* p. 75, n. 3; G. von Rad, *Old Testament Theology,* Vol. I, p. 42, n. 10.

24. So Helmer Ringgren, *The Messiah in the Old Testament,* Studies

in Biblical Theology, No. 18 (Alec R. Allenson, Inc., 1956), p. 15.

25. Johnson identifies the king as ritually the "suffering servant" and humiliated messiah; cf. *Sacral Kingship*, pp. 102–134, especially pp. 104 and 126; cf. also Ringgren, *The Messiah*, pp. 54–64. For the opposing view, see Mowinckel, *op. cit.*, p. 86, and nn. 5 and 6; G. von Rad, *Old Testament Theology*, Vol. I, p. 317, and n. 15.

26. Cf. Johnson, *op. cit.*, p. 102.

27. Cf. *ibid.*, pp. 328–329.

28. So G. von Rad, *Old Testament Theology*, Vol. I, p. 321.

29. On what follows relative to the Deuteronomist's theology of history, compare G. von Rad, *Old Testament Theology*, Vol. I, pp. 334–347.

Chapter II. HEBREW PROPHECY AND MESSIANIC KINGSHIP

1. Cf. James Muilenburg, "The History of the Religion of Israel," *The Interpreter's Bible: The Holy Scriptures in the King James and Revised Standard Versions*, ed. by George A. Buttrick, *et al.* (Abingdon Press, 1951–1957), Vol. I, pp. 319–321.

2. The analogy of Hosea's marriage, without which his book is incoherent, argues strongly for his authorship of its message of hope for the future. Most of the references to Judah, however, are demonstrably the work of another hand. Cf. John Mauchline, "Introduction and Exegesis" to The Book of Hosea, *The Interpreter's Bible*, Vol. VI, and Muilenburg, *loc. cit.*

3. Noth, *op. cit.*, pp. 264–265.

4. Cf. R. B. Y. Scott, "Introduction and Exegesis" to The Book of Isaiah, chs. 1 Through 39, *The Interpreter's Bible*, Vol. V, pp. 151–381. For some of the literature of the controversy regarding authorship and meaning, see Mowinckel, *op. cit.*, notes on pp. 102–110 and n. 2, p. 17.

5. There is no foreseeable end of debate over the authorship of the several eschatological oracles traditionally ascribed to Isaiah. Evidence frequently proves inconclusive. Certain of the oracles are demonstrably not Isaianic. Some can be ruled out because they presuppose the occurrence of events that actually transpired long after Isaiah's time: for example, the fall of Tyre in 332 B.C. (Isa. 23:15-18) and the exile of Judah in Babylon (Shinar) (Isa. 11:11 f.). Others can be ruled out on linguistic grounds; those of Isa., chs. 24 to 27, e.g., are almost universally dated after the Babylonian exile. Recent research in Oriental literature, however, makes precarious the rejection of any solely on grounds of their eschatological messianism. Cf. Muilenburg, *loc. cit.*, p. 323.

6. But note that Jeremiah's authorship is denied by Herbert G. May, "Introduction and Exegesis" to The Book of Ezekiel, *The Interpreter's Bible*, Vol. VI, p. 49.

7. For some of the literature of this debate, see J. P. Hyatt, "Introduction and Exegesis" to The Book of Jeremiah, *The Interpreter's Bible*, Vol. V, p. 988. Cf. also his remarks upon Jer. 33:15-16 in the same work.

8. Cf. May, *loc. cit.*, pp. 59 f.

9. For literature relative to the originality of the oracles to the nations, see May, *loc. cit.*, pp. 200, 217, *et passim*.

10. For some of the literature on this controversy, see May, *loc. cit.*, pp. 48, 244–245, 251, 256, 259–260, 266, 270, 272.

11. Cf. Walther Eichrodt, *Theology of the Old Testament*, Vol. I, tr. by J. A. Baker (The Westminster Press, 1961), pp. 59–60. For literature on this controversy, see May, *loc. cit.*, p. 270; see also pp. 54, 66, 251, 314, *et passim*.

12. Cf. Noth, *op. cit.*, p. 301.

13. Cf. Eichrodt, *op. cit.*, p. 127.

14. Cf. the translation by J. M. P. Smith, *The Complete Bible: An American Translation*, ed. by J. M. P. Smith and Edgar J. Goodspeed (The University of Chicago Press, 1939).

15. Whether or not, with Muilenburg and Skinner, we take the licking of dust from the feet as "an extravagant but thoroughly Oriental metaphor for self-humiliation," Hebrew anger and arrogance shine through. Cf. *The Interpreter's Bible, ad loc.*

16. Note that Isa. 42:5-9 and 49:7, 8-13 "should probably be added" to the Suffering Servant Songs, according to Walther Zimmerli and Joachim Jeremias, *The Servant of God*, Studies in Biblical Theology, No. 20 (Alec R. Allenson, Inc., 1957), p. 24, n. 63.

17. Cf. G. von Rad, *Old Testament Theology*, Vol. II, *The Theology of Israel's Prophetic Traditions*, tr. by D. M. G. Stalker (Harper & Row, Publishers, Inc., 1965), pp. 250 f.

18. For something of the history and present status of the controversy, see Zimmerli and Jeremias, *op. cit.*, pp. 23–25, and the Bibliography, p. 105. See also Johannes Lindblom, *The Servant Songs in Deutero-Isaiah*, Lunds Universitets Arsskrift, N. F. Avd. 1, Bd. 47, Nr. 5 (Lund: C. W. K. Gleerup, n. d.), pp. 94 ff. and 103.

19. Cf. G. von Rad, *Old Testament Theology*, Vol. II, p. 261, nn. 42–43; also, Zimmerli and Jeremias, *op. cit.*, p. 31, n. 98.

20. Cf. John Bright, *The Kingdom of God* (Abingdon-Cokesbury Press, 1953), pp. 150–151; G. von Rad, *Old Testament Theology*, Vol. II, p. 260; and Zimmerli and Jeremias, *op. cit.*, p. 25, nn. 69–70.

21. Cf. Joseph Klausner, *The Messianic Idea in Israel* (The Macmillan Company, 1955), p. 185, n. 1, and G. von Rad, *Old Testament Theology*, Vol. I, p. 86.

22. Cf. G. von Rad, *ibid.*, p. 85.

23. A reconstructed outline of the contents of Haggai, together with a selected bibliography, are offered by D. Winton Thomas, *The Interpreter's Bible*, Vol. VI, p. 1039.

24. For some of the literature dealing with the authorship of Zechariah, see Klausner, *op. cit.*, pp. 197–200, noting his own singular views.

25. On the import of this first appearance of Satan in Old Testament literature, see Thomas, *loc. cit.*, p. 1055.

26. Compare the reconstructed order of the text with that of G. von Rad, *Old Testament Theology*, Vol. II, p. 287, and of Thomas, *loc. cit.*, pp. 1071–1074.

27. Cf. G. von Rad, *Old Testament Theology*, Vol. II, p. 287.

28. Cf. Klausner, *op. cit.*, pp. 194–196, especially n. 14. Compare also Thomas, *loc. cit.*, pp. 1979–1981.

29. Cf. G. von Rad, *Old Testament Theology*, Vol. II, pp. 281–282.

30. Cf. *ibid.*, p. 288.

Chapter III.   THE BEGINNINGS OF ECCLESIASTIC MESSIANISM

1. Cf. Noth, *op. cit.*, p. 316.

2. For literature bearing upon the shift of royal functions to the hands of the high priest, see G. von Rad, *Old Testament Theology*, Vol. I, p. 249, n. 145.

3. On the usual assumption that the Chronicler not only wrote I and II Chronicles but also compiled and edited the Ezra-Nehemiah material, his work is generally dated between 350 and 250 B.C. Noth, *op. cit.*, p. 319, places him as probably of the third century. W. A. L. Elmslie, following A. C. Welch, argues cogently if not conclusively that our author did not compile Ezra-Nehemiah and that he wrote the Chronicles possibly between 450 and 350 B.C. See his "Introduction" to I and II Chronicles, *The Interpreter's Bible*, Vol. III, pp. 345–346, and his exegetical note on II Chron. 36:22–23. For other literature on the work of the Chronicler, see G. von Rad, *Old Testament Theology*, Vol. I, p. 347, n. 1.

4. Raymond A. Bowman, "Introduction and Exegesis" to The Book of Ezra and The Book of Nehemiah, *The Interpreter's Bible*, Vol. III, pp. 555 and 563 ff. Bowman includes in the memoirs additionally Neh. 11:1-2; 12:27-43; 13:4-31.

5. See above, pp. 21, 29–30, 37–42.

6. Cf. G. von Rad, *Old Testament Theology*, Vol. I, p. 244.

7. That Zadokites actually stemmed from Levi is a debatable assumption. Cf. Eichrodt, *op. cit.*, Vol. I, p. 398. For some of the literature, see May's comments at Ezek. 44:15-31, *The Interpreter's Bible*, Vol. VI, pp. 310 f.

8. Cf. G. von Rad, *Old Testament Theology*, Vol. I, p. 351.

9. See Noth, *op. cit.*, p. 319, n. 4, and p. 320, n. 3; also, Bowman, *loc. cit.*, pp. 561–563.

10. Sabbath (literally "rest"), and circumcision, once discretionary observances, became preeminent confessional symbols in exile, because the sacrosanct cultus could not be practiced in a foreign and unclean land. Cf. Noth, *op. cit.*, pp. 297, 298.

11. Cf. Noth, *ibid.*, pp. 331 f.

12. Cf. G. von Rad, *Old Testament Theology*, Vol. I, pp. 78 f. Noth even places the probable origin of P both in Babylon, *op. cit.*, p. 298, and in Palestine, *ibid.*, p. 336.

13. Noth, *ibid.*, pp. 335 f.

14. Noth, *ibid.*, looks to Lev., chs. 17 to 26, or Lev., chs. 1 to 7 and 11 to 15, for legislation deriving possibly from Ezra's code.

15. For recent estimates of the extent of P, see G. von Rad, *Old Testament Theology*, Vol. I, p. 77 and n. 18. For bibliographies relative to P in the general setting of the Hexateuch, see *ibid.*, p. 232, n. 96, and the suggestions at the end of C. A. Simpson's article, "The Growth of the Hexateuch," in *The Interpreter's Bible*, Vol. I, p. 200.

16. Cf. G. von Rad, *Old Testament Theology*, Vol. I, p. 249.

17. For a brief history of covenant theology, see Eichrodt, *op. cit.*, Vol. I, pp. 45–69.

18. If the assumptions of W. O. E. Oesterley concerning the original Hebrew text are correct, Sirach, variously called "Ecclesiasticus," "The Wisdom of Jesus the Son of Sirach," etc., should properly be entitled "The Wisdom of Ben Sira." Cf. R. H. Charles, *et al.*, eds., *The Apocrypha and Pseudepigrapha of the Old Testament in English*, 2 vols. (Oxford: Clarendon Press, 1913), Vol. I, p. 270.

19. G. von Rad observes: "We do not know from what date the Zadokites regarded themselves as the legitimate descendants of Aaron. Ezekiel still designates the priesthood at Jerusalem as Zadokite (Ezek. 44:15), but P knows only of the Aaronites," *Old Testament Theology*, Vol. I, p. 249. Sirach's single explicit reference to Zadok (Sirach 51:12 [ix]), extant only in the Hebrew text, is regarded by Box as probably a somewhat later interpolation. Cf. Charles, *Apocrypha and Pseudepigrapha*, Vol. I, p. 27.

20. Klausner dates his work ca. 190–170 B.C.E., *op. cit.*, p. 251; Box, between 180–175 B.C., in Charles, *Apocrypha and Pseudepigrapha*, Vol. I, p. 293.

21. So the Hebrew text. The Greek has "Onias."

22. On Josephus' mistaken identification of Simon the Just as Simon I, *Jewish Antiquities* xii, sections 48, 157, see Ralph Marcus in the Loeb Classical Library (Harvard University Press), Vol. VII, Appendix B, pp. 732–736.

23. Klausner, *op. cit.*, p. 251, dates the book about 130–110 B.C.E. Oesterley assigns the work in its final form to the last quarter of the second century B.C. Cf. Charles, *Apocrypha and Pseudepigrapha,* Vol. I, p. 60.

24. See James Moffatt, " Introduction " to II Maccabees, in Charles, *Apocrypha and Pseudepigrapha,* Vol. I, pp. 128–129; also, Klausner, *op. cit.*, pp. 251, 262, n. 1.

25. Cf. Josephus, *Antiquities* xii, sections 138–146.

26. See the article on " *Zaddoukaios,*" by D. Rudolf Meyer, in Gerhard Kittel, ed., *Theologisches Wörterbuch zum Neuen Testament,* Bd. VII, Lieferung I (Bogen 1–4), S. 38 and n. 21. On the basis of Josephus, *Antiquities* xii, sections 237, 387, who speaks of the flight of Onias IV to Egypt and of subsequent Zadokite influence there, Meyer distinguishes the Zadokite and Aaronite lines. G. von Rad, *Old Testament Theology,* Vol. I, p. 249, regards Aaronite as a name assumed by the Zadokite remnant in Judah.

27. Josephus, *Antiquities* xvi, section 163.

28. Josephus, *The Jewish War* i, section 68 in the Loeb Classical Library (G. P. Putnam's Sons, 1927).

29. *Antiquities* xiii, sections 254–258.

30. *War* i, sections 64–66.

31. *Antiquities* xiii, section 249.

32. *War* i, section 67.

33. *Antiquities* xiii, section 288.

34. R. H. Charles argues persuasively that Pharisaic opposition to the Hasmonaeans started when Jonathan assumed the high priesthood in 153 B.C. See his comment upon Enoch 90:6-17, in *The Book of Enoch,* tr. and ed. by R. H. Charles (Oxford: Clarendon Press, 1912), p. 207. The evidence, however, is not conclusive.

35. Josephus, *Antiquities* xiii, sections 171–173. See also *War* ii, sections 119–166.

36. Cf. Noth, *op. cit.*, p. 374.

37. Cf. Josephus, *War* ii, sections 164–166, and *Antiquities* xiii, sections 297–298.

38. Noth, *op. cit.*, p. 374, n. 2, accepts Geiger's identification of Sadducees with the ancient Zadokites as not unlikely. Meyer, " *Zaddoukaios,*" *loc. cit.*, p. 41, holds otherwise.

39. See in the Loeb Classical Library, H. St. J. Thackeray's comment on Josephus, *War* ii, section 119, n. c.

40. Josephus mentions two distinct communities, one of which was celibate, the other not, *War* ii, sections 120–161; cf. also Klausner, *op. cit.*, p. 289, n. 26.

41. Josephus, *Antiquities* xiii, sections 288–296.

42. See Meyer, "*Zaddoukaios*," *loc. cit.*, p. 43, line 24; and the comment by Ralph Marcus in the Loeb Classical Library, on Josephus, *Antiquities* xiii, section 288, n. c.

43. Josephus, *Antiquities* xiii, section 296.

44. Josephus, *War* i, sections 70–84.

45. *Antiquities* xiii, section 320.

46. Cf. *ibid.*, xiii, sections 395–397.

47. Josephus, *War* i, section 85.

48. See *ibid.*, i, sections 86–98; *Antiquities* xiii, sections 372–383.

49. Josephus, *Antiquities* xiii, sections 405–422; *War* i, sections 107–117.

50. Josephus, *War* i, sections 120–158; parallels in *Antiquities* xiv, sections 4–79.

Chapter IV.   Apocalyptic Messianism

1. Cf. Arthur Jeffery, "Introduction and Exegesis" to The Book of Daniel, *The Interpreter's Bible*, Vol. VI, p. 344.

2. Compare Jeffery's article, *loc. cit.*, p. 345.

3. Cf. Jeffery, *ibid.*, pp. 346, 499.

4. Cf. Jeffery, *ibid.*, pp. 348–349.

5. Cf. Klausner, *op. cit.*, p. 222.

6. Cf. Noth, *op. cit.*, pp. 396 f.

7. Gerhard von Rad, *Theologie des Alten Testaments* (Munich: Chr. Kaiser Verlag, 1960), Bd. II, S. 120.

8. Cf. Noth, *op. cit.*, pp. 396 f.

9. The reference to the resurrection of the dead in Isa. 26:19 is part of a psalm (Ps. 26:7-19) dating from about the same time as Dan. 12:1-3. Cf. *The Interpreter's Bible*, exegesis of Isaiah, *in loc.* For a survey of the resurrection idea in Jewish literature, see Charles in comment on Enoch 50:1, *The Book of Enoch*, pp. 98–99.

10. Cf. Jeffery's exegesis on The Book of Daniel, *loc. cit.*, pp. 495, 496.

11. Cf. Charles, *The Book of Enoch*, p. xcv. For the evidence adduced, see pp. xcv–cx. His argument is briefly summarized in *Apocrypha and Pseudepigrapha*, Vol. II, pp. 180–185.

12. See especially Charles, *The Book of Enoch*, p. cviii, n. 1.

13. Cf. Charles, *ibid.*, pp. x, xi, and *Apocrypha and Pseudepigrapha*, Vol. II, p. 164; also, Klausner, *op. cit.*, pp. 277–301.

14. Charles argues on the basis of Enoch 90:6-3, 16, that "the sheep with the big horn" is Judas Maccabeus, who is still warring — hence that Sec. IV must antedate the latter's death; further that Sec. IV depends upon Sec. I in something like its present form, hence that the Book of Noah and the whole of Enoch, chs. 6 to 36, must be earlier

than 160 B.C. See his *Apocrypha and Pseudepigrapha*, Vol. II, pp. 179–181. Contrast Klausner, *op. cit.*, p. 277, who regards Enoch, chs. 1 to 36 and chs. 72 to 108, as either from the time of John Hyrcanus following his break with the Pharisees or from the time of Jannaeus Alexander (ca. 110–80 B.C.). For other literature treating of the date of this section, see H. H. Rowley, *The Relevance of the Apocalyptic* (Harper & Brothers, n.d.), pp. 79–80.

15. Charles, following Hoffman, identifies the seventy shepherds as angels to whom God committed the care of Israel after he destroyed Jerusalem. See his comments on Enoch 89:59 in *The Book of Enoch*, pp. 199–201. Klausner, *op. cit.*, p. 285 and n. 17, regards them as the seventy elders who led the nation until Hasmonaean times.

16. See n. 11 above.

17. Section V contains additionally, in chs. 106–107, a Noachian fragment; in ch. 105 a two-verse messianic bit that better fits with Sec. I; and in ch. 108 a very late exhortation to hope despite the long delay of the Kingdom's coming. Cf. Charles, *Apocrypha and Pseudepigrapha*, Vol. II, p. 171, and his comments below the respective chapters.

18. Cf. Charles, *The Book of Enoch*, pp. 218–222. Klausner regards chs. 1 to 36 and 91 to 108 as constituting the " Basic Document," attributable, presumably, to a single author (cf. *The Messianic Idea in Israel*, pp. 278–284). The weight of evidence would seem to lie rather with Charles.

19. The messianism of ch. 105, an isolated, two-verse fragment out of place in Enoch, chs. 91 to 104, fits with the outlook of Enoch, chs. 1 to 36. Cf. Charles, *Apocrypha and Pseudepigrapha*, Vol. II, p. 170, and his comment below the text.

20. For a survey of changing conceptions of Sheol in Hebrew and Jewish literature, see Charles in comment on Enoch 63:10, in *The Book of Enoch*, pp. 127–128.

21. The discovery at Qumran of fragments of all sections of Enoch except the Parables, or Similitudes, suggests that this section and the final redaction of the entire book may be the work of a Jew or a Jewish Christian of the first, possibly even of the second, century A.D. See J. T. Milik, *Ten Years of Discovery in the Wilderness of Judaea* (Alec R. Allenson, Inc., 1959), pp. 33–34.

22. Cf. Charles, *Apocrypha and Pseudepigrapha*, Vol. II, pp. 184–185.

23. Cf. Charles's comment on Enoch 37:5 with reference to the meaning of *parabolai*, in *The Book of Enoch*, p. 70.

24. Cf. Charles, *ibid.*, pp. 64–65.

25. Cf. Charles, *Apocrypha and Pseudepigrapha*, Vol. II, pp. 287–289.

26. See D. S. Russell, *The Method and Message of Jewish Apocalyptic, 200 B.C.–A.D. 100* (The Westminster Press, 1964), p. 55, nn. 3–5.

27. Cf. R. H. Charles, *The Testaments of the Twelve Patriarchs* (London: Adam and Charles Black, 1908), pp. li–liii, xcvii; also, his *Apocrypha and Pseudepigrapha,* Vol. II, pp. 289–290, 294.

28. Cf. *Test. of the Twelve Patriarchs,* pp. lii, 45–46.

29. *Ibid.,* pp. 64–65.

30. *Ibid.,* p. liii.

31. *Ibid.,* pp. lvii–lix.

32. *Ibid.,* pp. lxi–lxv.

33. For a survey of numerous positions taken in the current debate over the origin, construction, content, and dating of The Testaments of the Twelve Patriarchs, see Russell, *op. cit.,* pp. 56–57, 311–319.

34. See below, pp. 141–145.

35. See Russell, *op. cit.,* p. 311, n. 2, in reference to an article by T. W. Manson in the *Journal of Theological Studies,* Vol. XLVIII (Oxford, 1947), pp. 60 f.

36. Josephus, *Antiquities* xiv, sections 79, 96.

37. Compare especially the enthronement ritual attributed to Isaiah, in Isa. 11:1-9. See above, p. 58.

38 For a listing of abortive messianic uprisings motivated by the Davidic ideal, see Russell, *op. cit.,* p. 319.

39. Cf. G. B. Gray, "Introduction" to the Psalms of Solomon, in Charles, *Apocrypha and Pseudepigrapha,* Vol. II, pp. 625 ff.; Klausner, *op. cit.,* p. 317; Russell, *op. cit.,* p. 317.

40. Titles of the scrolls, and their abbreviations, here depend upon the translation of Geza Vermes, *The Dead Sea Scrolls in English* (Penguin Books, 1962), which is cited because of its wide availability. Lowercase Roman numerals specify columns in the scrolls; line numbers in the columns are not indicated. Arabic numerals in brackets indicate the pages of Vermes' translation. Thus, CR vi [81] indicates the Community Rule, column vi, page 81, of the English translation.

The reader should know that a more common system of citation begins with an Arabic numeral (indicating the cave in which the MS. was found), continues with the letter Q (for Qumran) and initial letters of the Hebrew title, followed by an indication of the column in lowercase Roman numerals and of the line in Arabic numerals. Thus 1QS vi, 12 specifies the Community Rule, column vi, line 12. 1QSa = the Messianic Rule; 1QM = the War Rule; 1QpHab = The Habakkuk Commentary; CD = the Cairo Damascus Document, or Damascus Rule; 1QH = the Hymns.

41. On the meaning of allusions to Damascus in this document, see Helmer Ringgren, *The Faith of Qumran: Theology of the Dead Sea Scrolls* (Fortress Press, 1963), pp. 43–44. As noted by Vermes, *op. cit.,*

p. 95, the unpublished Qumran fragments of this book correspond to an incomplete tenth-century copy, " Manuscript A," discovered in 1896–1897 in a storeroom (*genizah*) of an old Cairo synagogue. This copy is the basis of Vermes' translation through column viii, where the MS. ends; thereafter the translation depends upon the less reliable " Manuscript B," a twelfth-century copy of the same work discovered at the same place and time. Manuscript B variants from the text appear in brackets or footnotes in the translation.

42. Cf. Vermes, *op. cit.*, pp. 18–25, and John F. Priest, "Mebaqqer, Paquid, and the Messiah," *Journal of Biblical Literature*, LXXXI, Part I (1962), p. 58, n. 9.

43. For further description of the method, see J. T. Milik, *op. cit.*, p. 40.

44. Vermes infers, *op. cit.*, pp. 42–44, that the Essenes used a calendar other than that of the dominant Jerusalem party, a conclusion bearing upon calendaric problems in the New Testament.

45. Equivalent to 1QSa ii, 12.

46. 1QSa ii, 14, 20.

47. Equivalent to 1QS ix, 11. On the expectation of two Messiahs, see Millar Burrows, *The Dead Sea Scrolls* (Viking Press, 1955), pp. 264–265; and Priest, *loc. cit.*, pp. 56 ff.

48. Cf. Milik, *op. cit.*, p. 126.

49. Cf. also CD vi [102–103], and the Comm. on Genesis xii [224].

50. Cf. Ezek. 45:7, 22; 46:2, 8, 12, 16; 48:21.

51. Equivalent to 1QSb v, 20–28.

52. Cf. Priest, *loc. cit.*, pp. 57 ff., and Milik, *op. cit.*, pp. 125–126, who also discusses the disconcerting confusion of messianic titles used in the medieval copies of the Damascus Rule.

53. H. H. Rowley argues, in *The Dead Sea Scrolls and the New Testament* (London: S.P.C.K., 1957), pp. 21–22, that the Essenes eventually allied themselves with the Zealots in the Jewish War of A.D. 64–70.

54. The Kittim, a symbolic name derived from Dan. 11:30 and Num. 24:23-24, are referred to also in WR xvi [144–145]; Comm. on Nahum i [232]; Comm. on Hab. iii, iv, vi [236–238].

55. So Burrows, *The Dead Sea Scrolls,* p. 223.

56. Vermes, *op. cit.*, pp. 53–55. See also Millar Burrows, *More Light on the Dead Sea Scrolls* (Viking Press, 1958), p. 299.

57. For surveys of such proposals, see Ringgren, *The Faith of Qumran,* pp. 38–40, and Vermes, *op. cit.*, pp. 57 ff.

58. See Vermes, *op. cit.*, p. 58. Ringgren, *The Faith of Qumran,* p. 41, proposes 170 to 63 B.C. as the outside limits, and rather before than after 100 B.C.

59. Cf. Burrows, *More Light,* pp. 194–201; also Vermes, *op. cit.,* p. 65. Ringgren, *The Faith of Qumran,* pp. 26–31, argues that both Seleucids and Romans were intended at various times.

Chapter V. NEW TESTAMENT MESSIANISM

1. On the prevalence of these presuppositions in current research, see Reginald H. Fuller, *The New Testament in Current Study* (Charles Scribner's Sons, 1962), pp. 73–75.

2. For the enunciation of these criteria, see Fuller, *ibid.,* p. 33.

3. Hans Conzelmann, "Jesus Christus," *Die Religion in Geschichte und Gegenwart,* Dritte Auflage (Tübingen: J. C. B. Mohr, 1959), Vol. III, cols. 629–633 especially.

4. Heinz Eduard Tödt, *The Son of Man in the Synoptic Tradition* (The Westminster Press, 1965), translated from the German by D. M. Barton, provides the most detailed critical analysis of the " Son of Man " sayings in current literature.

5. See the discussion above of the use of the title *Christos* in the same passage.

6. For contemporary arguments that the preaching of Jesus itself involved an implicit messianic understanding of his mission, see Fuller, *The New Testament in Current Study,* pp. 42–43, 80–82, *et passim.*

7. Cf. Reginald H. Fuller, *The Foundations of New Testament Christology* (Charles Scribner's Sons, 1965), pp. 108 ff., for a more recent survey of findings relative to the use of seven messianic titles in the Synoptic traditions.

8. Cf. Fuller, *The New Testament in Current Study,* pp. 36 f.

9. The meager results of form-critical studies for our knowledge of the historical Jesus, as of the decade of 1920, are summarized by Rudolf Bultmann, "The Study of the Synoptic Gospels," in F. C. Grant, ed. and tr., *Form Criticism* (Willett, Clark & Company, 1934), pp. 70–74.

10. For brief surveys of findings arising from the new quest, the reader is referred again to Conzelmann's article, "Jesus Christus," and to Reginald Fuller, *The New Testament in Current Study,* pp. 25–53, and *The Foundations of New Testament Christology,* pp. 102–141.

11. For a critical study, see Joachim Jeremias, *The Parables of Jesus* (London: SCM Press, Ltd., 1954).

12. Cf. Fuller, *The New Testament in Current Study,* pp. 49 ff.

13. For a review of current discussions of the death of Jesus, see Fuller, *ibid.,* pp. 43–45.

14. See the discussion in Fuller, *ibid.,* pp. 44–45.

15. Cf. the discussion in Fuller, *ibid.,* pp. 76 ff.

16. Fuller, *ibid.,* pp. 78–79, attributes this view to W. Marxsen in *Der Evangelist Markus* (Göttingen: Vandenhoeck & Ruprecht, 1956).

17. On the probability that Isa. 9:2-7 was an enthronement oracle composed by Isaiah for the coronation of Ahaz or Hezekiah, see the exegesis of R. B. Y. Scott, *The Interpreter's Bible,* Vol. V, pp. 231–234.

18. Cf. the language of the enthronement liturgy preserved in Ps. 2:7, " You are my son, today I have begotten you."

19. Martin Luther, " *Tractatus de libertate christiana,*" *Werke,* Kritische Gesammtausgabe (Weimar: Herman B. Nachfolger, 1897), Vol. VII, p. 66, line 35.

Index